W9-DCC-131

Reading *Grumble Hallelujah* is like having coffee with a wise, warm, honest friend when you're having a horrible day. I felt both understood and challenged in just the right combination—like Caryn has been there, like she can help me get to a better place.

SHAUNA NIEQUIST, author of *Cold Tangerines* and *Bittersweet*

Grumble Hallelujah is an authentic book about what it means to thrive in the daily-ness of life. Through its pages you'll be inspired to live with an expectant, open heart.

MARY DEMUTH, author of *Thin Places*

I feel indebted to Caryn Rivadeneira. Her accessible wisdom and vulnerability make us all more brave.

SHAYNE MOORE, author of *Global Soccer Mom*

Grumble Hallelujah is for those of us who sometimes wish we could trade in our lives like we might trade in an old, beat-up Chevy. It delivers the gentle, humorous, kick-in-the-pants reminder that the imperfect life we've been given—with all its dents, smells, and rumblings—is exactly the one we've been praying for all along.

EILEEN BUTTON, columnist and author of *The Waiting Place*

Genuine humility, refreshing honesty, and a tremendous sense of humor: a trifecta of qualities as powerful as it is rare in the communion of the saints. Blessedly, Caryn possesses this magical combination and expresses it with a well-earned gravitas in *Grumble Hallelujah*.

CATHLEEN FALSANI, author of *Sin Boldly* and *Dude Abides*

Caryn is honest and open about the challenges of life, and rather than try to fix it up all shiny and happy, she just sits with you on the kitchen floor and admits that life is tough. Her story has made all the difference to me as I grumble along!

TRACEY BIANCHI, author of *Green Mama*

Caryn has given us an honest, "no guilt" guide to letting go of fear and disappointment, to finding joy in the midst of struggles.

KERI WYATT KENT, author of *Breathe*, *Rest*, and *Deeper into the Word*

Grumble Hallelujah will challenge you to love the life God has for you, not with trite clichés or easy answers, but from a woman who displays the grace and mercy of one who is desperately seeking to live like Jesus . . . even in the grumbling.

JENNI CATRON, executive director, Cross Point Church, Nashville, www.crosspoint.tv

Grumble Hallelujah won't magically transform your life into a perfect one, but it will transform *you*, so that you more fully embrace and appreciate the entirety of who you are, imperfections and all.

HELEN LEE, author of *The Missional Mom*

Caryn tugs at my heart in a way I didn't expect. She is fearlessly vulnerable, and pushes us to be too. She speaks the language of letting go, a language most women struggle to learn. If you want to change the way you live, learn a "new hallelujah" from Caryn.

ANITA LUSTREA, *Midday Connection* executive producer/cohost; author of *What Women Tell Me*

With many personal stories, lots of laughs and precision incision, Caryn will open your eyes and heart to the reality and the results of your grumbling. Then she leads into practical and realistic responses that will change your attitude, reactions—even your life. *Grumble hallelujah*!

JUDY DOUGLASS, director of women's resources, Campus Crusade for Christ

Caryn has written a stellar book. And not just because it's honest and funny and dead-on about the disappointments and triumphs of life. It's fantastic because it's what I wish someone would whisper to me on those days when I just want to be someone else for a while.

CARLA BARNHILL, author of *The Myth of the Perfect Mother*; cocreator, The Mommy Revolution

From the beginning of *Grumble Hallelujah*, Caryn Rivadeneira reminds us—convinces us even—that God can be found in fear; in dark and gunky corners; and in our real, exposed lives. I love this deeply joyful, deeply honest book.

JENNIFER GRANT, journalist; author of *Love You More*

Many of us experience heartbreaking rough patches on life's road. *Grumble Hallelujah* arrives with comfort, humor, and grace for life's unwelcome terrain.

MELINDA SCHMIDT, *Midday Connection* cohost; coeditor, *Tending the Soul*

In this engaging, laugh-out-loud grumble-logue, Caryn walks us through her own sewer-water-in-the-basement moments. She's written a realistic, hopeful owner's manual for anyone wanting Jesus' abundant life when God holds back the goodies.

JONALYN GRACE FINCHER, vice president and speaker, Soulation; author of *Ruby Slippers*

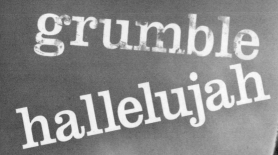

grumble hallelujah

LEARNING TO
LOVE YOUR LIFE
EVEN WHEN IT
LETS YOU DOWN

Caryn Dahlstrand Rivadeneira

· · · · · · · · · ·

Tyndale House Publishers, Inc., Carol Stream, Illinois

Visit Tyndale online at www.tyndale.com.

Visit the author's website at www.carynrivadeneira.com.

TYNDALE and Tyndale's quill logo are registered trademarks of Tyndale House Publishers, Inc.

Grumble Hallelujah: Learning to Love Your Life Even When It Lets You Down

Designed by Beth Sparkman

Published in association with the literary agency of Alive Communications, Inc., 7680 Goddard St., #200, Colorado Springs, CO 80920, www.alivecommunications.com.

Library of Congress Cataloging-in-Publication Data

Rivadeneira, Caryn Dahlstrand.
    Grumble hallelujah : learning to love your life even when it lets you down / Caryn Dahlstrand Rivadeneira.
        p. cm.
    Includes bibliographical references.
    ISBN 978-1-4143-3801-9 (sc)
1. Christian women—Religious life. 2. Attitude (Psychology)—Religious aspects—Christianity. 3. Optimism. I. Title.
    BV4527.R57 2011
    248.8'43—dc22   2011015993

Printed in the United States of America

17   16   15   14   13   12   11
7   6   5   4   3   2   1

To Rafi—
Thanks for sharing this life.
And putting up with my grumbling.
I love you.

Contents

Introduction

CONFESSION: If you'd have told me a few years back, as I lay on the kitchen floor, a sobbing, weepy mess, that I'd be peddling advice on how to love the life you're living, I'd have laughed in your face. Or, to be more honest, I'd have thrown a shoe at it. Which is what I nearly did to my husband, Rafi, when he stumbled upon me (quite literally) on the floor that day.

Instead, when Rafi knelt down and asked, "Caryn, what's wrong?" I hissed back, "I hate my life."

As soon as those words swung back around to my own ears, I realized I didn't *quite* mean them; however, they were the best I could come up with to describe the way I felt after three years of financial devastation and family stress; three years of disappointment, hurt, loss, anger, and confusion; and three years of feeling altogether forgotten by God. Nothing in my life was as it was supposed to be—and I hated that.

But here's the thing: while I wouldn't have believed you right then, if you'd have told me that just a few moments *after* my sort of dark midafternoon-of-the-soul experience I'd have something to say about loving life, I'd have paid attention. Because that's about the time God started working on me, touching my heart, opening my eyes, and convicting me of things that frankly I was in no mood to be convicted of.

Just when I wanted to settle into comfy self-pity and well-worn martyrdom, God started bringing things to mind: songs I loved, verses I underlined and could recite (well, *paraphrase* might be the better word), words I had scribbled in journals as an angst-filled teenager. All things that pointed back to what my attitude needed to be in those moments. In the midst of chaos and frustration. In the throes of hurt and loss. In that wilderness that my life had become. In that place where God had always been—even if it wasn't where I'd asked God to put me or ever imagined I'd be. I had to start saying "Hallelujah Anyhow," as that old song goes.

Over the days, weeks, and months that followed, I discovered that God welcomed my resigned, crabby, sigh-filled, grumbly hallelujahs. So I needed to learn to mumble it, grumble it, hiss it, or smirk it and learn to love the life God had for me even as my parents' marriage crumbled; even as my childhood home was sold and relics from my childhood—wanted only by me—piled up on shelves in my garage; even as my husband's business disintegrated; even as our financial situation devastated us; even as our medical bills piled up; even as relationships soured; even as depression shook its ugly gray cloak over my house; shoot, even as my beloved dog died. Even as I felt so alone. Even as there wasn't much to love about life, that's when and where I was to start loving it. And *rejoicing* in it. Ugh.

I just needed to know what loving my life really meant. It took awhile, but somewhere along the way I realized my former idea of loving life was all wrong. I had imagined it as some sort of puppy love. When things were going so well, when life was paying me all sorts of lovely attention, I'd sigh, sit with my head in my hands, and bat my eyes at life. Oh, how I loved it! Until it let me down. Then I fell out of love. In a hurry. My love was quite conditional.

Turns out, I had the wrong kind of love happening. The sort of love we need to feel for our lives runs deeper than mushy love letters. The love we should feel toward our lives is the same unconditional, "no matter what" love we feel toward our spouses, our kids, our siblings, our friends, our parents, and our pets.

It sounds crazy—until we realize that this love is the same because it's the love born out of gratitude that allows us to cherish and to value, to recognize worth. Just as I love my kids because they are like no one else and because God gave them to me, I need to love my life because no one else gets to live it and because God created it—ordained it!—just for me.

But for a long time, I had a lot of junk piled up (not only in my garage!) that kept me from loving this life. Which brought me here—to the writing. To figure this out.

So, if you're like me, if you've felt the loss of a life you loved or the life that was supposed to be or if you've had your own dark midafternoon of the soul and would like to know how to love your life, I hope you'll walk with me a bit here in the coming pages.

Before we go further, I want you to know a couple of things:

1. I'm not sitting here writing this from a place of "everything's great now!" I won't tell you just to think positively and smile more (though that can't *hurt*) and everything will work out well. Honestly, circumstances haven't really changed since my dark midafternoon of the soul—in many ways, they're actually worse. My parents didn't reconcile. Depression still lurks. Relationships suffer. Debt deepens. And, yes, that dog's still dead. So essentially, I'm still working with a lot of the same junk that got me there on the floor.

   I want you to know this because I know how annoying it is for someone whose life is suddenly perfect—all situations rectified—to talk about how to love life and be shouting hallelujah all the livelong day. That's not me. But a few other important things *have* changed: my perspective; my understanding of God; my experience of his faithfulness; and my idea of what loving life looks like, what it means. And that's huge.

2. I'm no Pollyanna. I don't wake up with a song in my heart or one coming from the little baby bluebirds chirping outside my window. In sharp contrast to a friend of mine who once told me the first thing in her head every morning when she woke up is, *I love being a mom. I have a great life!* the first thing in my head every morning is, *Morning already? You've got to be kidding!* or its cousin, *Can't these kids sleep?!*

   And I don't believe in Pollyanna-ish advice—or that happiness, per se, is our end goal. I agree with Charles Schultz (the *Peanuts* creator): "Happiness *is* a warm puppy" (emphasis mine). This means it's wonderful when it's there, and it's to be cherished for sure, but happiness is fleeting. It snuggles up for a while, but inevitably that happy puppy jumps right off your lap. It might even nip at you and dribble some pee on its way down.

This may sound harsh, but I don't believe in happiness as an end goal because I'm not sure that it's God's end goal for us. I rarely see God working things out simply so we can be happy. I think he wants us to be *holy*, as I'm sure you've heard before. So sure, moments of sheer happiness exist—hence the warm-puppy thing—but life isn't always rosy (even though he lived a perfect life, Jesus didn't strike me as a particularly chipper guy, to be honest). And I've learned that I don't really want it to be. God's got some good stuff for us in the not-so-rosy times too.

The thing is: loving anything—a life included—is hard work. It takes perseverance and discipline—some honest looks and hard choices now and again. So what we'll work through here isn't jolly or easy (though I will try to make this somewhat fun). But it's worth it—it's what the path to loving a crazy life is all about.

3. This one's a biggie. If your "hate my life" moment has come because you're trapped in a life of addiction or debilitating depression (or other mental illness) or abuse or some sort of danger, or if you hate your life so much that you have considered *ending* it, you need to hold off on this particular journey for a bit. We'll still

be here, waiting for you, but you need a specific path, one that offers help I cannot. Please make a phone call or shoot an e-mail to a professional who can help you. Then come back and we'll press on together.

And just where are we pressing on to? Well, I've broken the book into parts; each includes a chapter about something we need to get rid of (think, detox) and a couple of things we need to add (think, nourish) before we can learn to love our lives.

The first stop is oh, so cheery. We're going to grieve a bit for the life we imagined—or once had. I think it's okay to admit where we are isn't *exactly* what we had in mind. And I think God can handle that. So that's what we'll do in the next chapter.

Then we'll work on wringing out the other toxins that keep us too choked and tangled to love life—all that junk we hold on to that gets in the way of us loving our lives and keeps us from living as God intended us to—and finally we'll work on soaking in all the good stuff.

All of this is intended to help us love the lives God's given us and keep our hallelujahs going—no matter how they come out.

Sound good? All right. Let's go. Let's grumble.

PART I
Grumble Hallelujah

CHAPTER I

LIVE GRUMBLY

Letting Go of the Life That Was "Supposed to Be"

YEARS AGO, when the whole hanging chad debacle ended Al Gore's shot at the White House, my husband and I snuggled together on our brand-new sofa in our brand-new house (well, new to us) watching the news on our brand-new TV as we did nearly every night in our pre-kid life. And we talked about how sad this was for Al Gore.

Though, to be honest, I remember feeling less *sad* for Al and more *pity.* I pitied him in the way only someone whose life is going exactly according to plan—with many dreams fulfilled or ready to be grasped—can pity another person. It's that horrible, smug kind of pity, which I used to feel a lot back in those easy days.

But whether it was sadness or pity, I *felt* for Al Gore because he was "a man widely believed to have been groomed for the U.S. presidency from birth."[1] Meaning, his presidential aspirations weren't simply born out of the "Boy, you could even grow up and be president" sort of way many of us hear (with or without the "boy" part)—but that nobody actually believes will happen.

His dreams came from being the son of a "Washington insider." Young Al was sent to the right schools, surrounded by the right people, and even kept from playing the wrong instruments. (Talk about a political-stage mom: Mrs. Gore apparently made Al quit violin because "future world leaders do not play the violin."[2] Whoa, boy.)

Anyway, you see my point: Al Gore's life was *supposed* to go a certain way. And for many years it did. I imagine that he was all smiles during his vice presidency under the popular Bill Clinton (and if we're honest, he probably had his fingers crossed during those impeachment hearings!). Everything had lined up in his favor; his presidential destiny was right there—a tiny finger stretch away—his for the grabbing.

Then came the day—after months of lawsuits and recounts and Supreme Court hearings—when he realized he had lost his bid, lost hold of his destiny. It was then that I remember saying to my husband (and here's the point of this little walk down election-memory lane): "Aw, man. He's gonna need to grieve this."

So you'd think that several years down the pike, when my own life started unraveling—when my own life became pitiful—that I'd have remembered this "gonna need to grieve" piece of wisdom I so handily offered up to Al Gore.

But I didn't. I like to think that centuries of Swedish blood pulsing through my veins kept that from happening. It was as if every bit of my staunch ancestors' DNA yelled up to my brain: *Don't go there! We don't do grief! You know how we like it—bury it deep, keep it down, and just move forward! And for goodness sake, don't talk about it! Now get back to work.*

This is precisely why, even now, even when I know better, when I know that my dear beloved ancestors didn't have it exactly right, I'm so loathe to dive into this chapter. Grieving doesn't come naturally to me. If it does to you, awesome! You're already way ahead of the curve.

Grief is an essential part of the human experience, and God works wonders through it.

But I hate it. I hate entering into pain and processing it. So why do it? Why do I think grieving the life we miss or the one we wish we had is the first thing we need to do as part of our "detox" program? Why is it step one in learning to love our lives? Because grief is an essential part of the human experience, and because in our grief, God works wonders.

Why Grieve

Before you go nuts and catch me on technicalities, I'm not saying that grief itself is a toxin. But unacknowledged or un-dealt-with grief totally is (in fact, I believe it leads to some of the toxins we'll work on in upcoming chapters). We need to admit when life has gone astray or even all wrong. We need to acknowledge—cry out to God!—when life disappoints, when something important gets lost, and when we hurt because of it.

And we need to give ourselves (and others) permission to grieve the loss of dreams, of the life we thought we'd have, of roles we longed for, of relationships we thought would always exist, or whatever we desired but haven't gotten.

For a long time, I didn't think I had permission to do this. I didn't think it was right. I suppose I thought it was *sinful*. Because while we certainly understand the need to grieve the "big stuff" of life—like death or divorce or infertility—for much of the rest of it, grieving seems to run contrary to a good Christian life. It's not easy to admit we're a bit down because we're grieving a loss as "silly" as not having the family we imagined or the job we always wanted or, say, the income or lifestyle we thought we'd have.

And yet, if I'm being totally honest, I have to admit that much of the "stuff" that got me on the floor during my dark midafternoon of the soul was related to exactly that: to money, to our "reversal of fortunes." My life wasn't supposed to be about debt. About business loss or free-falling income. A person like me (raised in a well-off home, educated, and equipped with a work ethic to shame the Puritans) who was married to a man (smart as they come, with a knack for taking risks that paid off in only-in-America types of reward) wasn't supposed to live day to day, worried about mortgage payments on a modest home or how we'd get new summer clothes for the kids. A visit to the grocery store wasn't supposed to stress me out, as I wondered if my credit card would be rejected.

But could I grieve this?

So what about the other big "not supposed to be's" of my life during that period? Could I grieve the loss of picture-perfect holidays at my childhood home because of my parents' divorce? The loss of security—emotional and financial—within my own marriage? My loneliness and lack of meaningful friendships?

I mean, no matter how hurtful my grievances are to me personally, when we consider the vast scope of world problems, they hardly top the list. Could a good Christian girl really *grieve* the supposed-to-be's of life without being a big whiner?

You might ask yourself the same sorts of questions: What about the things that bring pain in your own life? What about those dreams you once had that now seem impossible? What about the life—or lifestyle—you thought you'd be living? Does God want you to grieve these things?

Could a good Christian girl really grieve the supposed-to-be's of life without being a big whiner?

Left to my own devices, I'd still listen to the voices of my stoic ancestors. But I couldn't shake a pretty basic truth: God doesn't want me listening to my *ancestors*. God wants me listening to *him*. So to the Bible I went. But while I searched, I also tossed out the challenge to some friends. I asked for examples from the Bible of people who grieved over, not the big tragedies, but the more banal supposed-to-be's of life.

Turns out, my friends are smart people. They suggested everyone from the obvious Naomi and Job (who grieved losses of *everything!*) to Moses grieving not being able to enter the Promised Land to Rachel grieving a pregnancy she had been desperate to have. Some of the grief made sense, some seemed weird, but all of it made me realize how patient our God is. And the good that grief can do when placed in God's hands.

Bible Grievers

God

"Does the Lord count?" Janine asked in response to my Great Grievers of the Bible Challenge.

Um, yeah. I hadn't thought of him as a griever, but I'd say he counts. Wouldn't you?

So Janine wrote back: "Well, the Lord grieved over making humans in the first place, and he grieved over making Saul king."

Righty-o! Check out these passages, with my helpful emphases:

> *The LORD saw how great man's wickedness on the earth had become, and that every inclination of the thoughts of his heart was only evil all the time. The Lord was* grieved *that he had made man on the earth, and his heart was filled with pain.* (Genesis 6:5-6, NIV, emphasis mine)

> *The word of the LORD came to Samuel: "I am* grieved *that I have made Saul king, because he has turned away from me and has not carried out my instructions." Samuel was troubled, and he cried out to the LORD all that night.* (1 Samuel 15:10-11, NIV, emphasis mine)

So if God grieved, it must be okay, right? It's an actual image-bearing thing to do, in fact. While the fall of humankind and rampant wickedness that God grieved could probably be classified as a "big thing," when you read it from the perspective of the Creator watching everything go all wrong, it begins to look a lot like what grieving was supposed to be.

Certainly, that's what was going on with Saul. He wasn't *supposed* to turn into a king who followed his own ways instead of God's. Hence, the regret and disappointment on God's part. (Of course, what's peculiar is that our omniscient God must have seen this coming, but that's a whole other conversation.)

I wrote earlier that grieving is an essential part of the *human* experience, but clearly, it's also an essential part of the *God* experience. A process in which something mighty happens. This helps explain (at least in my mind) one of the most bizarre grief sequences in Scripture: when Jesus weeps at his friend Lazarus's death.

I say this is bizarre because for days Jesus had been saying how Lazarus wouldn't end up dead. Then he tells Martha directly that he will raise her brother from the dead. Instead of being a "not supposed to be," this was a huge God-ordained event, a supposed-to-be if there ever was one! Jesus even said that Lazarus would be raised "for God's glory so that God's Son may be glorified through it" (John 11:4, NIV).

And yet, when our Jesus saw his dead friend, we know what happened (every former smart-aleck Sunday school student told to memorize their "favorite" verse can say it with me now): "Jesus wept" (John 11:35, NIV).

As bizarre as it might be, Jesus' grief just moments before miraculously raising his friend from the dead actually offers us a clue into what God-style grief can be about and how God uses grief to raise us up. We can't deny the grief-redemption or grief-resurrection connection.

Grieving, shedding tears, emptying ourselves of hurt seems to clear up room for God to work. While our grief may not allow us to raise friends from the dead, our grieving can bring other things—like peace, mercy, and joy—back to life.

Esau

When I first saw Esau's name on a friend's reply to my query, I thought, *What? Esau? Blech. No! Can't stand that guy.*

You know, he smells like a field (which sounds lovely, but since fields don't come with baths, I'm sure is not). He has hair like a goat. I picture him with blood and guts caked under his raggedy fingernails. Esau is just gross, right? And stupid—trading Jacob his birthright for some stew? So I ignored him.

But apparently, God didn't want him ignored. Because a couple of Sundays after writing him off, my pastor preached on Esau. About his grief, no less. About his agony of being stripped of his birthright and his father's blessing. And after Pastor Bert read Esau's heart-wrenching pleas and screams ("Bless me—me too, my father!" [Genesis 27:34, NIV] and "Do you have only one blessing, my father? Bless me too, my father!"[Genesis 27:38, NIV]) and after seeing this through a new lens, through my own pain and similar pleas with God, my heart changed for Esau. My heart broke for Esau, actually. When Pastor Bert described Esau's cry and pleas of "Bless me, too!" as the cry and plea of "a thousand have-nots in a world of haves,"[3] I was a goner for this guy. Oh, Esau.

After a lifetime of rolling my eyes at this goat-stinkin' man, I understood Esau. Totally. (I am a firstborn, after all. We have rights!) His life wasn't supposed to be about getting tricked out of his birthright—his inheritance, his home, his family, his future. But as it turned out, that's exactly what became of it. And he "wept aloud" (a.k.a. grieved) for the life he was supposed to have.

So what does God say about this kind of grief? We don't know exactly. But there's no mocking it. God doesn't seem to curse him for it—send plagues or ruin his life. In fact, quite the opposite. Because if we flip forward a few chapters to Genesis 33—after Jacob ran off to Uncle Laban's, married Leah and Rachel, grew rich, and wrestled with God, and after Esau found his own fortune—we see a reunion between these once-bitter rivals.

I love this story. Rightfully terrified of his brother's wrath, before heading home after probably twenty years, Jacob sends hundreds of goats, camels, cows, and donkeys as gifts to appease his brother. When they finally see each other, Jacob bows to the ground in humility. Genesis 33:4 (NIV) says, "But Esau ran to meet Jacob and embraced him; he threw his arms around his neck and kissed him. And they wept."

Then Esau asks about the kids and tries to refuse the gifts of the animals (in one of those gracious "oh, you didn't have to!" declines). Esau didn't need them—he was rich himself.

Finally, after all the denials and smiles comes my favorite line. Jacob tells Esau, "If I have found favor in your eyes, accept this gift from me. For *to see your face is like seeing the face of God*, now that you have received me favorably" (v. 10, NIV, emphasis mine). Ah, yeah. Jacob experiences grace from his big brother—and sees the face of God.

Now I hate to read too much into this—and granted, many years have gone by—but don't you think that Esau's grief—his crying out to God, his frustrated yells of "bless me too, father!"—helped get him to this place where he could offer grace? We don't see much of what happened between Esau and God in this story. But it seems that maybe his honest, raw response to getting gypped out of what was supposed to be his helped this broken human show the face of God to his brother.

I could go on and on, dipping deep into the stories of many of God's children who were disappointed, hurt, and grieved. But attention spans flicker, and we've got more to get to, so let me just point to two other quick places.

The Lamenter

When Jeremiah (mostly likely it was him, at least) wrote Lamentations, he, along with the rest of his nation, was having a rough go of things, to say the least. The Lamenter's life stinks, and he's letting God know it. Throughout this poem he lambasts God for such things as walling him in, chaining him down, piercing his heart, and breaking his teeth with gravel. I'd be lamenting too.

Don't you think that Esau's grief—his crying out to God, his frustrated yells of "bless me too, father!"—helped get him to this place where he could offer grace?

But the part that really gets me in this book goes like this: "I have been deprived of peace; I have forgotten what prosperity is. So I say, 'My splendor is gone and all that I had hoped from the LORD'" (Lamentations 3:17-18, NIV).

Here's what's so great. Not only is this guy grieving his (and Israel's) supposed to be's, but just after he writes—for God and the world to see—these devastating words of lost dreams and hope in God, he adds this:

I remember my affliction and my wandering,
   the bitterness and the gall.
I well remember them,
   and my soul is downcast within me.
Yet this I call to mind
   and therefore I have hope:
Because of the LORD's great love we are not consumed,
   for his compassions never fail.
They are new every morning;
   great is your faithfulness. (vv. 19-23, NIV)

Could it be then that this writer, like Esau, got to this amazing place of recognizing God's goodness through his grief? Could it have been his searing and beautiful cries to God that ended up sweetening his bitterness and soothing his gall?

When he remembers the pain of his life, he's still sad—he tells us so—but he is "not consumed." Aaah. Out of his grief comes one of the great treasures of Scripture: "Great is his faithfulness; his mercies begin afresh each morning."

The Lamenter offers us a lovely contrast to some other famous "wanderers" of the Bible. When the Lamenter's forefathers and foremothers grumbled and grieved in the desert after God miraculously delivered them from the Egyptians, they didn't give him even a smidgen of glory. The wandering Israelites refused to acknowledge God's goodness and faithfulness in their hardship. Unlike them, the Lamenter gives us words—glorious language—to express our frustrations in a way that still honors and recognizes our great God.

The Grumbler

The Lamenter got me thinking about something that had troubled me every time I considered the "godliness" of grief. One of my all-time, hands-down favorite passages is this:

> *Though the fig tree does not bud*
> *   and there are no grapes on the vines,*
> *though the olive crop fails*
> *   and the fields produce no food,*
> *though there are no sheep in the pen*
> *   and no cattle in the stalls,*
> *yet I will rejoice in the LORD,*
> *   I will be joyful in God my Savior.*
> (Habakkuk 3:17-18, NIV)

I mean, seriously, how great is that?

I first underlined this word-gem in my Bible twenty-plus years ago. (So, okay, my nonbudding fig tree first represented the lack of boyfriends in my life. Feel free to roll your eyes.) Since then, however, I've reread it a zillion times. The images fly from the page, don't they? Our noses almost itch in the dry, barren vineyard; our eyes blink at the hay bits flitting around the empty stalls. Certainly, the troubling truth of the passage smacks us right upside the head: even when life doesn't turn out how it's supposed to be, we need to rejoice.

As much as I love this passage, it troubled me because it seemed to contradict all that I wanted to be true about grief. But after reading and praying about the Esau and Lamentations passages, I realized I needed to read backward, to see what came before it. Duh.

And wouldn't you know it? My favorite passage, this beautiful bit, comes at the end of a book with a structure like this: Habakkuk complains; God answers. Habakkuk complains again; God answers again. Only *then* does our man H get it. But even *then*, Habakkuk grumbles his hallelujah. You just know he does.

There seems to be something to this grief thing. Not only does God do it, but God uses it to clear our heads and make room for him. I've been knee-deep in the Old Testament for this, but check out what James—in the New Testament—has to say about this: "Grieve, mourn and wail. Change your laughter to mourning and your joy to gloom. Humble yourselves before the Lord, and he will lift you up" (James 4:9-10, NIV).

God uses grief to clear our heads and make room for him.

Huh.*

In his book *In Memoriam*, Henri Nouwen says this about the disciples' extended period of grief after Jesus ascended: "This long period of mourning was necessary before they were able to receive the Spirit. Only after this long and painful grief were they able to receive the great consolation that their Lord had promised them. For it was only after they had given up clinging to their Lord that his Spirit could descend into their hearts."[4]

Go figure. This is just what James says. And this is exactly what we see lived out in Esau, Jeremiah, and Habakkuk—not

---

* What would it look like if we took James seriously and prayed this way? To help us find out, I've written a "Grumble Hallelujah" prayer and placed it at the end of every chapter. I invite you to personalize each one and make it your own. I hope, like me, you experience God's peace as you speak honestly about your disappointments and hopefully about his plans for your life.

to mention Sarai, Naomi, Job, and many others. They grieved, mourned, and wailed—and were lifted up. They experienced long and painful grief and were able to receive consolation from God. Being lifted up and consoled by our God are two keys to loving our lives.

Who doesn't want that? I know I do. So does this mean we need to grieve and mourn and wail every little disappointment of life? I don't think so, but let's move on to the next chapter and see if we can't figure something out.

OKAY, GOD:

I didn't want life to be this way. This isn't how it was supposed to be. At all. And I'm kind of mad that you have the power to change this—to make it right—but you haven't stepped in to make things different, better. But because I love you and I know you love me, I'm going to try to trust that you'll help me make sense of this disappointment. Thank you for walking with me. And for the many good things that are in my imperfect life.

Anyhow, God, Hallelujah.

Amen.

Getting to Hallelujah
Questions for Reflection and Discussion

1. How "Christian" do you think it is to grieve disappointments in life? Why do you think that way?

2. What are the things—disappointments or hurts—about your life that have made you think, *This is not how it's supposed to be?*

3. What are some of the things you've grieved in your life?

4. How have you seen God at work in that grief? How have you felt him lift you up?

5. What are some ways you have grieved or ways you need to grieve?

CHAPTER 2

LIVE BROKEN

Letting Go of Whatever's Holding You Together

FOR A FEW YEARS NOW I've wondered just how I got to this chaotic, messy place that is my life—a place that looks nothing like it was supposed to. Still, when it came time to write this chapter, I realized I hadn't had the real need to grieve for a while. And so I panicked. I didn't want this to be my *poseur* chapter—just as we're getting to know one another and all.

So I prayed that God would help me tap back into those places of hurt and anger and disappointment, to let me *feel* again so I could write honestly and vulnerably—and not from some obnoxious high horse.

Remind me not to pray that again. Because God—in his infinite, if maddening, wisdom—did one better. A couple of mornings after I prayed that, my mom came by to share some painful, icky junk about her and my dad's impending divorce. Stuff I didn't want to know (I keep strict boundaries in all this), but at the time it seemed I had to know because, well, it involved me and some "misunderstandings."

After my mom left, I called my dad for his side of things. It all disintegrated into a not-so-honoring-my-father, duke-it-out phone conversation with him. After we hung up, I was all fired up, huffing and puffing around my house, confident in my fighting "ready" stance, which I've gotten quite good at through the years. It's always good to be ready for the next shot, I figure.

But then, I caught myself—my eyebrows scrunched, my chest thrust out, my elbows bent, my hands in closed fists—in the dining room mirror, the one that hung above my parents' dining room table when I was a kid. Just then I realized something: my posture was all wrong.

As I stared into that mirror, the image changed. It was me, age five, sitting on the buffet table below it, a towel wrapped around my shoulders, my dad pulling my wet hair into horns at the top of my head. Us laughing. Me and my dad. Happy. My family. Together.

My heart broke.

I stared into the mirror longer, until I could almost see God's warm face, his sad, crooked grin, as I heard, *Grieve this.* I definitely felt his arm below me as I sank to the floor.

Because this bit of news was a reminder: the deep hurt in my broken, ailing family wasn't something to fight, but something to *grieve.*

And I knew it because of that heartbreak. For me, as cheesy or honky-tonk or seventh grade as this sounds, what breaks my heart is a wonderful trigger in knowing *what* I need to grieve. It's one of the emotions that separates the simple disappointments in my life from the big not-supposed-to-be's.

While I'm sure there are a zillion different, perfectly good litmus tests for determining what you ought to grieve (and you should use whatever works for you), in the course of my whining and complaining, I've singled out three different situations or emotions that tell me when I need to fight the "bury it deep" instinct and go ahead and grieve. Let's take a quick look.

What breaks my heart is a wonderful trigger in knowing what I need to grieve.

What Breaks Your Heart

This litmus test first occurred to me during the sudden, jarring death of my beloved (if totally insane) dog, Rocky, a number of years ago. His death kicked off what I at first dubbed my *annus horribilis* (a term meaning "horrible year" that I stole from Queen Elizabeth II). In fact, Rocky's out-of-the-blue death at only five—while I was seven months pregnant with our second child, when we were just weeks away from moving into our new home and just a week away from celebrating my baby brother's wedding—seemed to spark the flames that would engulf the way my life was supposed to be.

But of course, I didn't know this that day, when I searched my bookshelves looking for an answer to my question: Would Rocky, the Rocknose Monster, be waiting for me in heaven? Was the cheeseball-if-tear-jerking "Rainbow Bridge" poem (which every dog lover I knew e-mailed me following his death) correct? Was Rocknose waiting to meet me on the other side of the River Jordan? I grabbed book after book—dog books, theological books, a book of poems written by authors' dogs. (Yes, I have this. Don't laugh. It's fantastic.) But midquest, I stopped at this paragraph in the "introduction" to James Herriot's *Favorite Dog Stories*: "It is always said that however many wonderful and happy years a dog lives, you know that one day, the day he dies, your dog will break your heart."[5]

That was it. That was the emotion. My dog had broken my heart. And it hurt like crazy. Besides giving me permission to grieve (which I didn't exactly need, since grieving a dog's death is acceptable, I think, according to our cultural sensibilities), it did two other things for me. One, I realized that I hadn't really had a broken heart before, which seemed crazy, since I'd had my share of doomed relationships. But two, and more important, it named the feeling and allowed it to become a recognizable benchmark for the years to come.

At first, though, I was no good at recognizing this—even as the heartbreaks started piling on. With God's help, however, I learned to take these as cues to grieve.

And I've found that what breaks my heart can be personal things—like my parents' divorce or my own marriage stressors. Or it can be a friend's or family member's things—for a friend and her sick child or my own child's pain. Or it can be horrifying and tragic things—like my friend getting shot by his brother-in-law and losing his wife and unborn baby at the hands of the same man. Or it can be more global things—like the injustices of this broken world, children going hungry, women being brutalized, all the inequity, all the suffering.

In fact, I've gotten to the point where I realize my heart should be broken nearly all the time. Because I believe God's is. Recognizing this emotion not only tells us when to grieve, but can signal us to action.

God's heartbreak for his fallen world set in motion a plan for rescue. I believe that God is close to us in our heartbreak (Psalm 34:18), not only to help us grieve and heal us, but also to orchestrate some rescue operations.

My son recently stormed out of our TV room during a commercial for an animal rescue organization.

"I can't stand to see their sad eyes," he said as he left.

Of course, that's exactly the point of the commercials. Call it manipulation if you like, but the proper response, I believe, of the human heart is to feel the break and move to want to help. To call and make a donation to help end animal abuse or neglect. Or to feed a hungry child. Or to hug a hurting friend. Or to cry out to God in your own pain.

I realize my heart should be broken nearly all the time. Because I believe God's is.

What You've Lost

The parables of the lost sheep and the lost coin (Luke 15:1-10) have always gotten to me—though probably for all the wrong reasons. While Jesus told these stories to illustrate the unrelenting love of God for his lost children—and I get that—I also tap right into the sentimental fool element of the stories.

I understand that the shepherd and the woman searched high and low for a sheep and a coin because losing them had tough financial implications. However, the rejoicing that happens at the end of these passages seems to have more behind it than simply the cash registers "ka-ching-ing" in their brains (case in point: both spent some money celebrating the finds!). The truth is, finding something precious that was lost zaps you with ecstasy. That rush from despair to relief once you find something is a luxurious emotion.

What, then, if we've lost something precious and it's never found? Can't we assume the opposite is true? That we need to grieve what is lost?

I say, absolutely.

Of course, this area gets dicey. Because we don't want to end up grieving every lost library book or set of car keys. Sometimes, we just need to pay our fines, use our spares, and move on. But for the times when loss goes beyond annoyance or inconvenience, we need to admit that there's just something about loss. It stinks. And it can hurt. Whether it be the loss of something physical, something financial, or something emotional or relational. Whether it's about a lost opportunity, a lost love, or a lost cause. It's something to grieve.

For many of us, this is where the whole "it's not supposed to be this way" thing hits home.

We've reached points in our lives where we realize that many of the dreams we once had or the plans we mapped out have gotten lost—or at least we have. We've lost time or ability or energy and have had to leave behind things and ideas that mattered. Or we've misplaced them and can't for the life of us get them back.

This is what Esau grieved. He lost his birthright and everything to which he had been entitled. In Matthew, we read of Jesus' grief over what Jerusalem lost out on: "How often I have wanted to gather your children together as a hen protects her chicks beneath her wings, but you wouldn't let me" (Matthew 23:37). As a mom, I hear that it's not only Jerusalem that lost out, but Jesus, who lost the opportunity to snuggle and coddle his people. Women who have longed for children—or lost them—certainly understand another level of Jesus' ache here.

But something so cool happens when we admit and grieve our loss—or even before then. God swoops closer. Just before James writes about us being lifted up in our grief, he offers this lovely little line: "Come close to God, and God will come close to you" (James 4:8).

When we offer our grief to God, it's a way we come close to him. I often imagine myself scooting up to God, inching ever closer. Like my kids (and my dog) do with me on the sofa. In those moments, it's hard for me to be so near without reaching an arm around or stretching fingers forward to offer a pat or a scratch. So I suppose it is with God. When we come close, and scooch up to our Father, that's when we feel the swooping, the surrounding of our God who's there with us in our grief.

And God is good to have around—even when he's the one we're blaming for our sorrows. Because ultimately, nothing is lost on God. Literally. He knows where every*thing* is. He knows where every*one* is. While we may lose sight of dreams, of goals, or of God, he never loses sight of us or what he wants from and for us.

While this doesn't mean we'll miraculously get back the cherished family photo we lost in a flood or we'll recover a lost love or our lost dream will suddenly be fulfilled, God *is* a seeker and a restorer. That means he can take our losses, our hurts, and our missteps and restore them to blessings. He's good like that. We see him do it again and again in Scripture, from Esau and the folks we have discussed to the many we haven't. Think about the healings of the bleeding woman, the lepers, the demon possessed. Think of the horrors that God turned right around.

And if we're honest and look carefully, we see God doing the same in our own lives.

What You Cannot Change

So have I depressed you enough yet? If you weren't ready to grieve before, you're certainly getting close, huh? Sorry. But this is important to tackle. And we've got one last thing to address before we move on to some ways to grieve. We've got to talk about grieving the things we cannot change.

God is a seeker and a restorer. That means he can take our losses, our hurts, and our missteps and restore them to blessings.

I have to confess I stole this wording from a friend who once told me about her need to grieve the man she had married. He hadn't died. He simply wasn't the man she thought he was—or he acted like he was—before they married. During their marriage, she had discovered some personality *ick* that after years of praying about, she realized would probably never go away. He would probably never change.

My friend came to a point where she realized she could either gripe about it for the rest of her life and play the martyr, or she could grieve it and move on. "We all need to take time to grieve what we cannot change," she told me.

Her words flashed me back to a totally different conversation with a totally different friend. After discovering that their last child would be yet another boy, my friend's mother-in-law told her to "go ahead and grieve the daughter you won't have." At the time, I thought this was horrid and cruel and crazy. What an awful thing to say to an expectant mother! What a horrible view of the sweet boy my friend carried! Right?

And yet, suddenly, it made more sense. If, in fact, my pregnant friend had hoped for a daughter (which, for what it's worth, she hadn't), it seemed reasonable to grieve that. It's not only something you cannot change—technically, it's also a loss. Maybe my friend's mother-in-law was on to something, after all.

The trick with this litmus test is discerning what falls into this category. We are told to—and should—hold out hope. And we know that God can work miracles and change even the most dire situations and the most stubborn people. But we also know he doesn't always. He doesn't, for example, seem to change baby boys into baby girls.

The discernment we need is described most beautifully and famously in Reinhold Niebuhr's "Serenity Prayer." It's now a staple of any 12-step program. Those of us who've spent any time in a 12-step program can almost certainly recite the first part of it:

God grant me the serenity
To accept the things I cannot change,
Courage to change the things I can;
And wisdom to know the difference.

When it comes to realizing, accepting, and then grieving the things that will never change, we need to take
them to God. After all, this wisdom—and serenity—comes
straight from God, from the Holy Spirit who gives us both
discernment and peace when we ask for it. We might not
get an e-mail from God saying, "Just do 'X' and relax,"
and we might not get peace about the things we wish were
true, but when we seek him and his will and his wisdom,
he grants us that serenity. I know. I've been there.

*It seems
like a weird
juxtaposition—
grief and hope—
and yet, in many
ways it is the
gospel.*

I've spent a lot of time over the past
several years praying for things that
haven't changed—and that are looking
like they probably won't. I've also spent
a lot of time frustrated with a God who
could point a finger and change hearts
and minds and rectify situations but who
doesn't, apparently.

Yet in all this, I've somehow gotten more crazy about the
God who chooses not to "fix" my parents but simply reminds
me to love them.

Again and again and again.

So when it comes to *things* that won't change—a broken
marriage, a dream whose time has expired, a life that disappoints—we need to change what we can in ourselves, and
then accept and grieve what we can't. We can grieve it in the
present and yet hold on to hope for the future. It seems like a
weird juxtaposition—grief and hope—and yet, in many ways
it is the gospel.

OKAY, GOD:

What can I say? My heart aches. I feel like so much has been lost—or taken—from me. And there's so much I want to change that I just can't. When I allow myself to feel all this, I'm overwhelmed with grief. It's hard to feel any joy in life. And yet I know you're here with me. Help me to feel you, to sense you close. Thank you for being willing to step into this dark, lonely place with me. And for knowing how this feels.

Anyhow, God, Hallelujah.

Amen.

Getting to Hallelujah

Questions for Reflection and Discussion

1. How naturally does grieving come to you? Do you mourn disappointments easily?

2. What are some of the litmus tests you have for what or when you need to grieve?

3. What things about your life break your heart?

4. What are some of the specific things about life that you feel you've lost?

5. What are things you cannot change no matter how much you long to?

CHAPTER 3

LIVE BLUBBERY

Letting Go of the Tough-Girl Act

IF I'M HONEST, one of my major hang-ups with the grieving process is the *image* of grief. Specifically, I can't forget one snapshot that took root in my memory probably twenty years ago when I attended a funeral for an elderly man. His way-grown, almost-elderly-herself daughter sprawled her torso across and her arms around the casket just before they lowered it into the grave, and she started wailing. Spooky wailing. "Daddy, no! Daddy, no! Don't go. Don't go," echoed through the cemetery.

When I think *grief*, my brain pulls up that sight and those sounds. While this might be an understandable response at a beloved's funeral, it's not exactly the grief response we need for what breaks our hearts, for what we lose, or for what cannot change. I'm not saying it can't be, but remember that Swedish DNA gurgling around inside me? Well, it kind of makes me recoil at this sort of grieving. This is going to make

31

me seem pretty mean, but honestly, my brain almost always drowns out this haunting memory with Ella Fitzgerald singing the Gershwins'

> *Stiff upper lip, stout fella*
> *Carry on, old fluff*
> *Chin up, keep muddling through*[6]

While "stiff upper lip" may be an English saying, we Swedes know how to rock a stiff lip as well. But to be fair to my ancestors—and my DNA—this isn't their fault. I don't think my reaction to extreme grief has as much to do with my *Swedish* DNA as with my general *human* DNA— the stuff that allows us to make it through hard times. You know: survival instincts.

It's natural for us to want to buck up and carry on when faced with adversity. . . . But in our culture, we take this a bit far.

I think it's *natural* for us to want to buck up and carry on when faced with adversity. Don't freak out, here. I'm not going all Darwin on you, but God did equip us—emotionally, physically, and spiritually—to endure, to survive. I believe he made us this way so we could live (maybe even enjoy) life and be purposeful. So it is good that we can respond to crises or difficult times with our chins up and carry on.

But in our culture, we take this a bit far. I read an article recently that let my ancestors off the hook even more. The writer, a pastor named Bob Hyatt, wrote "Don't Forget to Grieve" for the *Out of Ur* blog—and it's a lovely meditation on why we ought to grieve on Good Friday (and Holy Saturday, for that matter) and why "every worship service shouldn't be a celebration." He started the piece by recounting his experience at church the Sunday after September 11, 2001.

Hyatt had longed for the first Sunday after the devastating event to be a churchwide mourning and questioning session. Instead, he writes, "I was asked to salute the flag and sing the 'Battle Hymn of the Republic.' What I needed was a church service. What I got was a pep rally. We needed to grieve. Instead, we were told to feel better."

He adds: "And we wonder why so many of us struggle with a persistent, low-level depression. Maybe, just maybe, it's because when we should, we refuse to grieve. We hold in the tears, when they should come out. That emotion tends to leak out in other ways, at other times—some not nearly so appropriate or healthy as crying."[7]

I sometimes wonder if this is the reason why "denial" is considered the first stage of grief. But still, once we know *what* we need to grieve, we need grieving tools in our arsenal—ones that work for us, with our personalities, and ones that allow us to feel and "process" the emotion.

I'm going to plunk through a few of the ways that I grieve. Again, you need to find ways that work for you. I should also mention that none of these have a specific time limit attached—it's not like I cry one moment and *whammo!* I'm over it. Sometimes, actually, that does work, but often, it's just one step of the process. Sometimes I work through all these examples. Sometimes it just takes time. But here are some thoughts on *how* to grieve.

Cry

This may shock you: when you feel sad, when you're grieving, cry. It helps. What? You think this is *obvious*? Okay.
Fair enough. Seems like the benefits of crying weren't lost
on some of our heroes of the faith, certainly not on Hannah
nor on David. Not on the entire nation of Israel while they
were enslaved in Egypt. Not on Nehemiah nor even Mary
of Bethany. Oh, and not on Jesus, of course.

All right. So maybe it's obvious for most people, but
honestly, this one was pretty new for me. Up until my dark
midafternoon of the soul, I could have counted on one hand the
number of times in my life I'd cried out of grief. I don't remember crying when my grandmothers died. Not because I didn't
love and miss them, but because I just didn't. I don't remember
crying when friends moved away. Same thing. Just didn't.

If you had asked my *Farmor** if she cried when she emi-
grated from Sweden to America at sixteen, she would've
looked at you like you were nuts. Because of this, my mom
always thought Farmor *was* nuts, or at least that she must've
been pretty "emotionally dead."

Maybe Farmor was—but then maybe so was I. Because
I totally got why Farmor didn't cry. Not only because a little
thing like moving to a new country at sixteen didn't seem so
bad when you'd essentially been sold to another farm at age
ten to support your family and endured who knows what
sorts of horrors, but because some things in life just require
that stiff upper lip. Farmor was busy surviving; she had no
time to cry.

---

*Farmor is Swedish for "father's mother." Don't say I never taught you anything!

And yet, there are plenty of times to cry. Even my tough-as-nails Farmor shed some tears eventually; I'm sure of it. Even though I never saw her do it.

We all know how good a cry can feel. According to William H. Frey, a biochemist at the University of Minnesota, we feel "'better' after crying due to the elimination of hormones associated with stress, specifically adrenocorticotropic hormone." In other words, we relax. When you mix this with tears, it leads to a theory that "crying is a mechanism developed in humans to dispose of this stress hormone when levels grow too high."[8]

Even though I have no idea what adrenocorticotropic hormones are, Dr. Frey's idea makes perfect sense to me. From a purely immediate emotion-release standpoint, sinking into a good cry seems to clear the mind, heart, and soul a bit. It's just getting there that can be difficult—for some of us, at least.

I know many of you cry at every Hallmark commercial. But that's a different type of cry, I think. Speaking for myself, when it comes to crying for the things that grieve me, I need to find time and space. Now that I've become an actual crier (though the only commercials I cry over are sad dog ones), I have to give myself this or else I end up crying over ridiculous things—in an irresponsible way.

When I'm feeling the need to cry out my grief, I find a space to be alone—sometimes it's in my office, sometimes it's in the shower, often it's in front of the sink, doing dishes (no one ever seems to join me in this task . . .), sometimes (though rarely) it's out for a walk. If I know I need to cry, but the tears don't come, I provoke them. Shamelessly. I get the sad music flowing. The John Denver station on Pandora works wonders. Or I'll read a sad poem.[9] Or I'll meditate on a particularly sad psalm. There are a lot of them. Singing an old, sad hymn can get the tears streaming easily enough too.

It sounds sappy and maybe even insincere, but it often takes some coaxing to move from crazy-busy-survival-mode Caryn to a version of me who can relax and feel and grieve and cry.

In that same *Out of Ur* post on grieving, Bob Hyatt contends that our inability to grieve and cry keeps us from fully experiencing joy as well. And it's true. If we can't exhibit the depths of pain by intentionally sinking into our grief, feeling it deep in every molecule and letting the tears tumble, neither can we fully share the heights of our joy, arms held upward and out, spinning and smiling in delight.

Lament

Lamenting—expressing sorrow or mourning "demonstratively," according to Merriam-Webster[10]—is my favorite form of grieving. I love yelling at God, waving my arms and carrying on a bit. Well, usually I don't actually yell as much as whisper near-obscenities at him or huff and cluck my tongue or just *think* mean thoughts toward God. But I love to let him know how he's messing up my life.

If we can't exhibit the depths of pain, neither can we fully share the heights of our joy.

Some might question the wisdom of this, but it's biblical. Not only do we see this in the book of Lamentations, but how about Habakkuk? Remember him? The guy who wrote my favorite passage ever?

My pastor-friend Gregg recently described this book of Habakkuk as "The Difficult Dialogue."

"Sometimes it's appropriate to shout and sing hallelujah," Pastor Gregg said. "Other times to lament and complain."[11] Had I gotten to him first, he might have even said "grumble."

It can be difficult to wrap our brains around the idea that our complaining and grumbling honor God. Since he's after honest connection and conversation, though, he seems to honor it. As we discussed in the last chapter, honest griping—from a place of deep grief or disappointment—seems to get us closer to God.

Later in that same service on Habakkuk, the band played, "Better than a Hallelujah." If you haven't heard it, you might just need to put this book down and Google it. Amy Grant recorded a version. Chapin Hartford and Sarah Hart wrote it.

The lyrics all ring true and lovely, but these words specifically pressed deep into my heart: "We pour out our misery/ God just hears a melody." The song goes on to say this is because these are "honest cries" from brokenhearted people. And that is what's "better than a Hallelujah."[12]

I'm not sure that honest cries are better than honest praises, but the point is that whatever we bring to God honestly and with our whole hearts sounds like a melody to him. God wants our hearts, whether they're broken, crabby, whiney, or filled-up and jolly. As long as we're sincere. How great is that? How great is our God?

But aside from spilling some truth into my own heartache, hearing this song did something else for me: It reminded me of one of my other favorite ways to grieve.

Create

This spring my mom, husband, three kids, and I attended an illustration class at Walt Disney World's Hollywood Studios. Our instructor had us all drawing Louis the Alligator from their recent movie *The Princess and the Frog.* He stood at the front of the class in front of this big, cool drafting table, with a drawing surface that projected onto a screen. We all sat at even bigger cool drafting tables with Mickey Mouse desk mats that held our papers in place. Then, the teacher began by showing us how to make proper circles by rotating our shoulders and not our elbows or wrists (who knew?), and took us from sketched circle, to semicircle, to swoopy line. Step-by-step till at the end of the twenty-five-minute class we all had alligators.

My mom's and husband's were really good. If you saw the movie, you would recognize their Louis the Alligator right away. My eight- and five-year-olds' were amazing too. These little kids could draw a couple of mean alligators. I was so proud.

And then there was mine. Or, the one I drew with my three-year-old, who didn't want to draw his own. So Fredrik just scribbled all over the paper he shared with me. Honestly, I think his scribbles improved my rendering. What I drew looked nothing like an alligator. Nothing like anything, actually, except a few bad circles, a bunch of weird lines, and some desperate attempts at "candy corn" teeth.

All this to say, everyone in my family can draw but me. And maybe my younger son. For whatever reason, I'm surrounded by people who can sketch and paint and who have nice penmanship. And who enjoy that.

Not me. I like to type.

However, just because I'm not—and never will be—an "artist" in the way most people conjure up the term doesn't mean I'm not one. I am creative. And I love to create. Creating—specifically the kind that can be done with my sweet little MacBook snuggled on my lap—is one of my favorite ways to grieve.

Especially angry creations. I write really well when I'm mad or hurt or disgusted or discouraged. The only thing I don't do well in these instances is hold *back* what I've written. The blogosphere is filled with a few too many of my angry, hasty rants. I don't regret writing these things—maybe just publishing them.

After many years as a "public" writer, I'm learning the power of private writing. And I've learned this specifically by getting back into poetry. Back when I was probably seven, poems (Shel Silverstein's poems to be exact) made me fall in love with words, sentences, and fragments—and the rhythm and sounds of them spoken together.

While this may be hard to believe coming from a woman like *moi*, who can ramble on and on about grief, I love the terse power of poetry, the challenge of working within tight form (of my own making), and tilling around for the right words. I even love the visual of poetry. It's as close to drawing as I'll ever get—and be decent at (because you can do it while typing). Writing poetry forces all my senses into action. Not one of them gets to be lazy, to hide in the back. And that's what makes it perfect for processing my grief.

That, plus I'd be hard-pressed to ever let another human read my poetry. Because I love poetry so, I also recognize that probably a good 99.9 percent of every poem ever written is schlock. Including mine. Which is why I spare the world.

All this to say (imagine if I'd have said this in a poem—we'd be done with the book by now!), whether you create best by drawing, writing, singing, acting, sculpting, cooking, gardening, hammering, painting, dancing, or yodeling, do it when you need to grieve.

Writing poetry forces all my senses into action. Not one of them gets to be lazy, to hide in the back. And that's what makes it perfect for processing my grief.

Two Sundays before he preached on Habakkuk, Pastor Gregg preached on Lamentations. (Job fell in between. Gotta love studying misery during Lent. What a great series this was!) Gregg described Lamentations as a book "where art and desperation meet."[13] Lovely, isn't it? And yet after I heard this, I kept wondering, when *don't* art and desperation meet? At least, when doesn't *good* art meet desperation?

God gave us art and creative abilities because we are made in his image and the first thing he was for us was our Creator. But I think art exists so that we can cry out, grieve, mourn, and understand what God is up to, just as much as it does to celebrate the wonders of this world. When you hear of artists "pouring" themselves into their art, it's the emotions—good or bad—that are being referred to. And often, I think desperation is what drives artists to their art. Whether a desperate love. A desperate ache. A desperate question. A desperate need.

Recently I had the opportunity to interview—and chat

a bit with—Susan Isaacs, the author of *Angry Conversations with God: A Snarky but Authentic Spiritual Memoir.* Take a wild guess what the book's about. Lamenting. Whining. Complaining. Because her life has not gone the way it was supposed to go. Sound at all familiar?

Because she's hilarious and so "authentic" and "snarky," naturally, I loved this book. It's a must-read for those of us who are grumbling our hallelujahs.

But anyway, in her book (and in the stand-up act that the book is based on) she shares some selections from her therapy session in which she takes God to marriage counseling. Yes. It's so great. Toward the end, in one session, she shares this (Rudy is her therapist):

SUSAN: I have to accept that God isn't going to give me the life I want: I may never get married, and I'll never make a living doing what I love.

RUDY: That's a big loss. I'm sorry.[14]

This may sound like a silly thing to quote. But here's what made me underline it: This came on page 221. After 220 pages of writing out her anger with God, she gets to the point where she can name and accept her loss and finally grieve it.

The whole book is a creative lament—not unlike Jeremiah's or Habakkuk's. (Well, hers isn't an acrostic or meant to be sung with stringed instruments. At least, I hope not.) And it moves her heart from angry conversation right to a place near the heart of God. All because she was angry, all because she was creative, and all because she sought God.

The value of a creative act like this—or like cooking or singing or knitting out your grief—can't be denied. Especially when it leaves you with something beautiful.

Move

My friend Nicole got some disappointing news awhile ago— that something she had been working hard toward wasn't going to materialize. She messaged me to tell me about it; I responded with a frowny emoticon and told her that I was shocked. She replied with this: "I'm going to be bummed about it today and then be better tomorrow."

Well, that seemed awfully hopeful, I thought. I might have taken a few more days to soak in my bummed-out-ed-ness about it.

But later that day, I noticed on Facebook that Nicole had gone for a run. Now she's one of those types of people I will *never* understand—the type who runs for fun and does it all the time—so she may have run because it was part of her life, but she may have done it that day because running makes her feel better. Running makes me hurt (and have to pee, actually), so I don't understand this, either. That said, though I hate to run, I do like a good walk. I love a long bike ride. I love lacing up my tap shoes and making sure I can still pull off a decent Rhythm Buck Time Step and still Shuffle Off to Buffalo. Whenever it is even remotely close to handy (which it hasn't been for more than ten years), I like to ride a horse as well.

All this to say, I do like to get my body moving. And I especially like to do so when I need to grieve. While no one would ever mistake me for an athlete, I do know there's a wonderful connection between the body, mind, and soul.

Even when the mind and soul seem to be stuck, getting our bodies moving and flowing—pushing our muscles beyond their comfort zones: feeling our hearts pound, our skin sweat, and lungs expand—seems to do something for us, and it goes beyond the adrenaline rush.

Moving seems to clear our minds and free our souls so we can name and claim what we need to grieve and then get that before God. Because until we can do that—until we can lay before him our grief, our pain, our hurt, our disappointments, our regrets, our frustrations—we can't see and love the life he has for us. And whether we know it or not right now—actually, whether I know it or not right now—it's a great life he's got in mind for us.

Even when the mind and soul seem to be stuck, getting our bodies moving and flowing seems to do something for us, and it goes beyond the adrenaline rush.

Go

So Chicago has this suburb called Naperville. Perhaps you've heard of it. Seriously. It's this monster of a town. (As I type, it's got 142,000 people living among its winding streets. By the time you read this, it'll have like a quarter million. Probably.) Naperville always tops those "Best Places to Live" and "Best Places to Raise Kids" lists. It's preppy and yuppie and has the Riverwalk and express trains into "the City" and is all sorts of lovely.

And yet, I shake my fist at it and curse its very name every time I get on the Eisenhower Expressway, which should be the fastest way to get me the fifteen miles east from my door to the city of Chicago. It should, in fact, take about twenty minutes. Thanks to Naperville*—which squats another fifteen or so miles southwest of my town—and its bazillion "we're the best!" residents who apparently also like to visit "the City" when I'm heading downtown, the trip usually takes an hour.

But that's not all Naperville means to me. The town always makes me a little sad. My mom grew up there—way back before it was chic. Back when it was a "hick" (as my mom called it) country town, surrounded by farms. Many of the townsfolk were well-enough off even then, but it also had sections of crazy poverty. One of these sections is still there—you'd just never know it. I doubt any of the "Best Places to Live" list folks ever see this area. But Naperville still has a small area of tumble-down, tiny shanties where once families of six, eight, and ten people squeezed in. Where alcoholism was rampant; where mental illness ran wild—so much that it seemed the norm. Where tragedy was woven into daily life and where escape was on everyone's mind.

Until we can lay before him our grief, our pain, our hurt, our disappointments, our regrets, our frustrations— we can't see and love the life he has for us.

This is the Naperville where my mom grew up. This is the birthplace of so much of my family's pain. So whenever I'm in that town, a sort of full-body sorrow sweeps through me. I find myself shaking my fists at the town again—for letting my mom fall through some cracks and making her ashamed when she didn't need to be.

---

*To be fair, Aurora also shares some of this blame. Wheaton and Winfield, too, probably. And Sugar Grove, I see you expanding. . . .

So, honestly, I spend as little time as possible there. Who needs to feel that way, right?

Why tell you all this? Because one recent morning I spoke at a church in Naperville (I didn't share my feelings on the town), and you gotta hear what God did: Two days before, I had written that sentence about not crying over my grandmothers' deaths. And I'd felt terrible about writing it ever since. It was on my mind all that weekend. So I prayed about it (because apparently, I didn't learn my lesson last time!). I asked God to give me tears if I still needed to cry about them. If it would help heal some long-buried wound or honor their legacies to me.

I honestly didn't think much about it when the speaker-coordinator for my event e-mailed me the night before I was to speak to give me directions to the church. It was on the main drag right through town, next to a hospital and a cemetery. So driving through downtown Naperville that morning, I felt the familiar heaviness sink over my body. Sad memories, heartbreaking stories, family regrets, all that stuff swelled in me. Then I saw the cemetery. Or I should say, *the* cemetery, where a grandfather I never knew, an aunt and uncle I rarely saw, and a grandmother I never grieved are all buried.

Just be glad you weren't near me on the road. Because, boy, did I cry. I saw the church parking lot up ahead and turned in, hardly able to see. I put my hands to my head, started wiping my eyes, and laughed through my tears. "Jesus! I didn't need to cry *now*." Apparently, he doesn't care that a speaker's mascara is toast or that she shows up with swollen eyes. So like Jesus.

I joke. But I think it's true. He doesn't care how our grief looks. He doesn't care that I was a bit of a wreck walking into that church, sniffling and glassy-eyed as I asked where the mothers' group met. I think he prefers us walking in like that, actually.

But *going* to grieve doesn't necessarily mean revisiting a sad place or the scene of the crime. It can be going to a person— the one who caused you grief or the one whom you need to grieve. Maybe it's a long-overdue visit you need to make or a talk you need to have. Maybe it's a picture you need to dig out or a home movie you need to watch. Maybe you need to friend somebody on Facebook so you can face that old hurt or fear and resolve that conflict.

Maybe you need to go to a place and a person. Maybe you need to kneel at someone's grave for a while. Maybe you need to weed around that tree planted in someone's honor. While I hear plenty of people rag on them, I think cemeteries and memorials are lovely things, because they force grief and allow misery.

And I think God is a fan of this. Frankly, I don't believe it was coincidence that I spoke at a church next to the cemetery where my grandma lies two days after I prayed that God would allow me to grieve her. I think God's serendipitous nature swirled the whole thing together.

Because I think God—like cemeteries—forces grief and fuels misery. Sometimes, at least. I think he likes us in the very places where hurt happened. Where people disappointed us. Where bad memories lurk. Where darkness dwells. Where life took that horrible turn. I think he likes us there because he is there. It's so often right where he's meeting us. Ready. Arms open. Chest warm and soft. Eager to envelop us, to let us sink into him and for him to sink into our sad, dark places and to bring them some light.

It's just the thing that can allow us to start loving and living this life God has for us.

But there's a kicker—one that I've faced down many times after a good cry. Often, after the final nose blow, after the tears have stopped, after the last line of the poem is written, or my anger at God has subsided, I may feel better, but a question lingers: "Where do I go now?"

Because grieving means we know we lost something but accept that we have to move on without it. This can terrify even the bravest of us. Leave us frozen right on the path we're meant to travel down.

I think he likes us in the very places where hurt happened.

But in my life, that same God who so warmly welcomes my raging, broken heart has encouraged my faltering feet as well. The thing about God is that he's here with us. In every place we are, at every place we need to go.

So we'll end our sniffling here and start wriggling in the next section.

OKAY, GOD:

All I've got for you right now is this: my tears; my anger; my big, hard questions. So take them. I offer you these angry, hurting words I've written, the despair I've created, each difficult step I take. Do with them what you will. Thanks for listening. Thanks for accepting my angry offering. Thanks for loving me even in my grief. I love you.

Anyhow, God, Hallelujah.

Amen.

Getting to Hallelujah
Questions for Reflection and Discussion

1. What is your natural response to grief?

2. Does grieving—in any form—come easily for you? Why or why not, do you suppose?

3. What sorts of things might you need to cry about?

4. How might lamenting—crying out to God!—help you process your grief?

5. What sorts of things do you create (think big!)? How do these things help you deal with your emotions?

6. In what ways have you experienced a body-soul connection through movement?

7. Where might you need to go in order to grieve? How frightening is it to think about going there?

PART II
Wriggle Hallelujah

CHAPTER 4

LIVE UNSTUCK

Letting Go of Fear and Control

YEARS AGO, I wrote an essay about being stuck in life. It went a little something like this:

> "Shoot," I said under my breath as I slid my daughter off my hip, jiggled the fishing pole into a better position, and maneuvered the stroller out of the way. I gave the bathroom door another hard shove with my shoulder. Nothing. "What a perfect end to this summer," I huffed. "Babygirl, looks like we're stuck in the loo."
>
> My three-year-old daughter, Greta, looked up at me with a bit of panic, and my pinched face did nothing to calm her. It wasn't that I thought we'd never escape (my husband and older son knew where we were). It was just that this stuck feeling, this sensation of my life going nowhere fast, which had dogged me all summer,

had come along on this vacation and morphed from feeling to reality, trapping me, Greta, and my baby, Fredrik, in the bathroom on Anderson's pier in Ephraim, Wisconsin.

The stuckiness, as I'd begun to call the feeling, first showed up in early summer after potty training Greta. While I was thrilled to have her out of diapers, getting two preschoolers to "go" before leaving the house only to have one of them need to go "for real this time!" after getting buckled into their car seats made me batty. Every trip to the pool, outing to Grandma's, and "quick run" to Target seemed to get stuck before it began.

Then stuckiness showed up in my work. Editing and writing projects—things I usually could pour my energy, heart, and mind into—would get jammed up in ways that had never happened before and seemed beyond my control to unstick. While I bounded with creativity and enthusiasm, it seemed at every idea, someone would say, "Great! But let's hold off."

And then the stuckiness got hold of my marriage. Just as my husband and I were getting back into the relationship groove after having our third child in five years, we hit some rough terrain and were having trouble pressing through it. No doubt my attitude, which was stuck in bad, tired, and martyr, didn't help.

And now this: Stuck in the bathroom. Stuck in self-pity. But more importantly, stuck with two little kids who were getting antsy to get out.[15]

The story—which itself ended up getting stuck in publishing purgatory for years (oh, God, you and that sense of humor of yours!)—ended happily enough. Another kick and shove, and the door opened and my kids and I were treated to an amazing view we might otherwise have missed. And that was the moral of the story. That God uses *stuckiness* "to give us focus, grow us, shape us, and recharge us."

And it's a good moral. Just maybe not quite a complete one. In the years since that experience, I've realized two things. One, when I wrote this I had that ridiculous, piteous thought that I was the only one in the world feeling this way. You know, because everybody else's lives always seem to be swimming along so fine and dandily. I didn't realize what a *major* impetus to life-grumbling my feeling of stuckiness was. I had no idea how many of us feel stuck. And how often we do. Learning that I was indeed not alone broadened my perspective a bit.

Two, back when I wrote the article, I was stuck in a place where I felt (and maybe rightfully so) that my stuckiness was no fault of my own. Or, to be clear, that it was all God's fault. I did cop to this a little bit when I wrapped up the article with: "I've learned a better technique for getting through: stop spinning, stop pushing, stop trying to get unstuck. Instead breathe in, breathe out, and wait—on God."

And that was good—and true. But I still wasn't admitting that sometimes—often, actually—we get *ourselves* stuck; we step right into the gook of life that gets us stuck. Sure, sometimes God uses gook too—to hold us in place. Probably more often, though, the reason we stay stuck isn't because we can't get rid of the "God gook" but because we won't get rid of our own gook.

What was funny was that the story itself helped me figure this out. Because in the years it spent floundering, waiting for the right home at the right time, my story realized it had no control over where it would end up, and then it started worrying that it might just die on the publishing-limbo vine. My poor little story *felt* stuck because of its control freakiness. Or, okay, so maybe it was me. But you get what I'm saying: I realized something new about "stuckiness." At least, as it goes down in my life.

More often than not, the junk that holds us back and keeps us stuck is our desire to be in control and our own fear.

And that is: if we want to get (or feel) unstuck, if we want to scrape off the gook that holds us back and holds us down, we have to know what the gook is. More often than not, that gook—the junk that holds us back and keeps us stuck—is our longing to be in control and our own fear. And we step in it all the time. Like we're looking for it.

If we want to keep from feeling stuck in life, we need to tackle these big issues. We need to learn what to do when we finally realize we're not in control and what to do when fear stares us down, freezing us in our tracks. Read on.

Outta Control

I admit it: I am a classic control freak. Well, at least for myself. I don't feel the need to control anybody else's lives—even my kids'. Despite the eye-rolling my mom and husband are doing as they read this, I'm happy to let most people be who they need to be and do what they need to do. But when it comes to me, I want to be in charge. To call the shots. And most of all, to make happen what I want *when* I want it to happen.

While this sounds perfectly reasonable to me, apparently, God's not great with this. Sure, he's good with the free will and the choices thing, but he really holds tight to *timing* issues, doesn't he? And that's where we start to feel stuck.

Never is this worse than when we're certain that God *wants* us to do something, be somewhere, use our gifts in a certain way—but yet we're forced to sit. Tight.

We're ready to go—chomping at the bit—and the gate just doesn't pull up for us. We're in the right place, but the door just won't budge. It's the perfect job, but the offer doesn't come. The idea and the writing are great, but the book proposal gets no after no after no. We're doing our part, but the relationship stays stale. We've made the improvements, but the home value stays in the toilet. Whatever. Fill in your own situation. But I'm talking about the experiences—or seasons—we enter into where we know we've got someplace we need to be, but by golly, we just can't make it happen! When we realize we are out of control. And stuck right there.

Of all the free will God affords us, he just doesn't give us power over timing. And God is rarely in a hurry. I often wonder why on earth Jesus didn't start preaching or performing miracles until he was thirty. It's not like he had a lot of time left!

But God doesn't view time the way we do. I have no idea how God views it, in fact. All I know is that we can't change the amount of time in a day, and we can't force others to do anything in our timing. And this is not for a lack of trying.

Take my daughter, Greta. She totally takes after my

husband when it comes to time. Which is to say, she operates on her own schedule and is usually late and unconcerned for how she might hold others up. As her mother, I have an idea that I can force her to hurry. That I can speed her up. That my clapping hands or threats of consequences will make her rush. Make her brush her teeth quicker. Make her tie her shoes faster.

Uh-uh. No can do.

I can encourage her. I can get her started earlier and create environments in which I know she operates at her speediest. But I cannot—no matter what I do—force her to move faster or slower. It's not up to me. Unless, that is, I want to turn from mother to puppet master and physically control her every move. And I don't. I just want her to be a bit more respectful of other people's (i.e., my) time. (So I guess I'm even more of a control freak than I thought!)

Regardless, I spend ridiculous amounts of time aggravated with her pokiness, muscles tense and tight because we're not walking out the door right when I say. I spend a lot of time feeling stuck because her sense of timing is not my own.

I'm sure some of you are coming up with all sorts of things to say about my parenting skills here, but the point is this: I'm never really stuck because she is slower than I am. The stuckiness is all my doing. Not hers. We still leave. We still get where we need to go. Usually just a minute or two later than I would have on my own. So was I ever really stuck? No. It's ridiculous to feel this way.

And yet, in other seasons of my life where the stuckiness has lasted longer than a couple of frustrating minutes—when it's been weeks or months or years—really, the same situation is happening. Just on a longer spectrum. In the course of *eternity* it's ridiculous to feel stuck just because things don't happen on our timetables. Right?

And yet we do—because, I think, we make ourselves feel stuck. Because we tense and tighten. Because we bang against doors for too long. Because we want things *now.* Because we have no idea how to simply wait—and chill.

A Facebook friend had this update today: "This morning I took a step in the direction I believe God is leading . . . let's see what happens! For the record, I hate waiting."

I'm laughing even as I reread this. It's ridiculous—her stepping where she believes God is leading, yet not trusting his timetable. Of course, I feel this way all the time. All the time! And it's why I feel stuck. I can pretty much guarantee that if God makes her wait for whatever this is, she'll feel stuck. She'll be grumbling about it on Facebook. As would I.

We hate to wait. We see no value in those times. Because it *feels* like doing nothing. And then we get antsy. So we fight and we force and we bang and we pull and we nag and we despair and we spin our wheels and we feel stuck.

The truth is, in the seasons of waiting and feeling stuck, God can be moving in us and around us more than ever. I mentioned earlier Jesus' long wait for ministry. While it might seem like a giant waste of thirty good God-on-earth years, obviously God was working on something. John the Baptist was out, preparing the way for sure. But other things were set in motion as well. Things that needed to happen, people who needed to *be* for his will to be done.

What if we could understand this, believe this to be true in our lives as well? Instead of pushing and forcing and trying to move, what if we did the opposite? What if—when we felt like we were moving forward (or whatever "direction" we felt God nudging us) or when we knew we were doing our best, doing what we were made (or told!) to do— as soon as we began to feel stuck, our first reaction was not to tense up and fight but to ease up and throw up our hands? What if instead of frantically looking for ways out and around, we looked for God, to see where he was in all this? What if we gave up control?

In the seasons of waiting and feeling stuck, God can be moving in us and around us more than ever.

A few Sundays ago, I wrote this down on my church bulletin: "When you're stuck . . . do nothing—wait for grace; look to the cross." I have no idea what the context was. I'm guessing our pastor said it. But I don't even remember.

Now that I've reread it a bunch of times, I sort of stumble over the churchy language (although, not to brag, but I am fluent in "church"). But I still like it. And I get it.

When we're stuck: Do nothing. Wait for grace. The grace to move forward. The grace to endure. The grace to look for what God is up to.

Fear Less

A while back, my friend Tracey and I met for lunch to discuss a project. While munching on our sandwiches and sipping Diet Cokes, we talked about "big issues" women face. "Fear" came up as one of them. We agreed it was a good one, and then the strangest thing happened.

I can't remember which one of us was first to say, "Well,

I mean, I'm not afraid." But the other joined in, quickly adding, "Oh, me neither. I'm not afraid of anything." Within moments, Tracey and I had morphed from grown women (each a mother of three!) into twelve-year-old boys, posturing, chests out, heads cocked, clucking our tongues as we tried to out "I'm not afraid" the other.

It was weird. But it was true. For the most part, I don't think of myself as a chicken. I'm not afraid—of much. I can read Stephen King in the dark, before bed, and sleep soundly. I can speak in front of crowds without butterflies. I throw my opinion into arenas where I know I'll take a beating. I pipe up and chime in, even when I know people may disagree. I write about things that might come back to haunt me (or at least embarrass my kids).

And Tracey, sheesh. She does all these things too—and she's a pastor! She preaches the Word of God, baptizes babies, conducts funerals, and has to, you know, *pastor* people. Yikes.

But then the twelve-year-old boys faded back into the grown women when one of us ventured, "Well . . . at least not for myself. I do get afraid when I think about the kids. . . ." Suddenly, we were both talking about the zillions of things we are in fact afraid of.

Speaking for myself, I fear that we haven't chosen the right school. I fear we'll have to move (and change schools) and scar my kids for life. I fear that we won't make enough money to provide for our kids. Writing this section on a plane (as I am right now) reminds me that I'm afraid of plane crashes— I never was before I had kids.

But with that doozy, my fears move away from parenting and right back to myself. I often fear that God is calling me to do something I don't think I can do. Or, even worse, I fear he'll stay silent and never call me to anything in particular. Or worse yet, that I won't hear—or heed—the calling.

I fear fading into the background. I fear insignificance and being forgotten. I fear the choices I make on my own. I fear I'll go right on back to feeling so distant from God. I fear that because I'm now a child of divorce, I'm more likely to get divorced myself. I fear what could happen if I were rich again. I fear we'll stay broke forever. I fear I'll lose my desire to change the world. I fear things will get dark again. I fear someone will stop by unexpectedly and see how messy my house is. I fear what other people think. I fear that I'll bother people. I fear—sometimes—that I'll lose my mind.

I can't forget my physical fears: I'm afraid of snakes, heights, and open-backed staircases. I could go on and on. I'm afraid of a lot.

And yet, the Bible says—God says!—do not be afraid. I once read that we're told this—not to fear—more than a hundred times in the Bible. According to a colleague of mine, "Fear is addressed a lot more frequently than, say, lust or pride."[16] Interesting. More than some *deadly* sins. Huh. And yet I am so often afraid. Perhaps God understands the deadliness of fear.

More than a hundred times in the Bible, we're told not to fear.

The other night when talking about this, someone told me, "God and fear cannot occupy the same space." I can't get that out of my head. I'm not sure it's right theologically. I mean, if I believe (and I do) that the Holy Spirit resides in me and that my body is the temple of God, I'm sure God occupies a space in me. And so does fear, often enough. (Especially now, in fact, since this flight I'm still on has gotten quite choppy!)

So I don't think the guy is right. I think God and fear *can* occupy the same space. But it's a ridiculous image. Picture it with me. Think of something that terrifies you. For me, that might be having to climb open-backed, snake-covered stairs on my way to my kids' new school because God has called me to something new.

Imagine the fearful thing or setting. Now imagine fear itself. For all it does to me and keeps me from, when I picture fear I see it as a shriveled-up brown thing. A stale raisin. A dried piece of dog poop. A tiny, burnt end of a fire-poking stick, coughing up sparks, dribbling smoke. You picture it however you like.

Now picture God next to it. Occupying the same space. Honestly, it makes me laugh. Even if you picture fear as giant and mighty and growling and grabby, how can it measure up next to God? God! Warm, strong, open, loving. Hands ready, arms wide and big, eyes smiling.

Even if you picture fear as giant and mighty and growling and grabby, how can it measure up next to God?

Of course, if your image of God is whacked-out, this might get tricky. If you picture God as aloof or uncaring or full of shrugs and with a "not my problem!" attitude then you've got a problem. You need to work on your image of God. You need to get to know the Big God, the Loving God, the Warrior God, the Hand-Holding God, the It-*Is*-My-Problem God. Yes, even the Footprints-in-the-Sand God! You need to know—and picture—the God who says these words:

> *When you pass through the waters,*
>   *I will be with you;*
> *and when you pass through the rivers,*
>   *they will not sweep over you.*
> *When you walk through the fire,*
>   *you will not be burned;*
>   *the flames will not set you ablaze.*
> *For I am the* LORD, *your God,*
>   *the Holy One of Israel, your Savior.*
> (Isaiah 43:2-3, NIV)

You need to picture the God who tells us this because "you are precious and honored in my sight" and "because I love you" (v. 4).

Truth is, I think that God *can* be in the same space as fear. But when you see he's there—big and mighty—next to shrively old fear, you're more likely to show fear the door. You're more likely to notice that nerve is eager to take its place.

Accepting that we're not in control and that we have nothing to fear frees us to experience something wonderful: that we're in the place God wants us. He may want us to step forward—sprint or leap forward, even! Or he may want us to wait. But if we're seeking his will, living obediently and patiently without fear, we can rest assured that he's up to something even when it feels as though we aren't doing a thing. It's in those moments that we realize we are not stuck but instead on a road to living mightily. Which is where we're headed next.

OKAY, GOD:

I'm sick of feeling stuck. Yes, maybe I'm scared. Or maybe I hate giving up control. But can't I start moving in some direction? Do you really want me to just sit here and wait? Well, even though it feels wrong, it feels like I'm no use, it feels like I'm wasting time, I'll try to trust you. Help me be unafraid. Help me hand over the reins. Help me to trust that you love me enough to have me stuck here for a while. And then, if you ask me to follow you into some hard places, thank you for your promise to walk with me through every raging river and blazing fire.

Anyhow, God, Hallelujah.

Amen.

Getting to Hallelujah

Questions for Reflection and Discussion

1. What situations or circumstances have made you feel stuck in life? What was your response to that feeling?

2. How much of a control freak would you say you are?

3. When are the times you feel most out of control?

4. What is your "normal" response to feeling out of control? Do you panic and try to reclaim it or do you "let go, let God"?

5. How about fear: what things or circumstances make you feel most afraid?

6. What's your normal response to fear? Do you freeze, flee, or fight?

7. How might learning to give up control a bit and be less enslaved to fear help you feel less stuck in life?

CHAPTER 5

LIVE MIGHTILY

Letting Go of Trepidation

THIS PAST MOTHER'S DAY my son Henrik and I watched a nature show (actually *Nature* was the name of the show) all about mama animals and their babies. One of our favorite parts featured a mama doe and her sweet baby deer. We learned lots. For example, did you know that to keep predators from smelling their blood and sniffing her new baby out, the normally vegetarian doe eats her baby's placenta? The poor thing literally gags it down. Watching the doe choke, shake her head, and stick out her tongue was at once sweet, gross, and laugh-out-loud funny. If you've spent any sort of time around kids, you'll understand why I think this is just like much of motherhood.

While I loved the placenta part best because my son laughed so hard, the thing that really grabbed me was the commentary about the innate fear that each deer is born with. We could see it right there on TV: as soon as the newborn deer was licked clean, she stood, quaking—as her mom gobbled and gagged on the afterbirth. Her blinking eyes roved the forest for things she'd never seen but knew to be terrified of.

Once Henrik stopped laughing at the doe's facial and neck placenta-induced convulsions, he worried about the baby. "She's so scared," Henrik said. "That's so sad!"

I agreed with him as he said this, but as I listened to the narrator, I wondered if her quaking was really all that sad. Because the newborn deer's innate fear is what sparks her "flight" response—which is what all deer have to keep them safe. Deer don't have huge, ripping teeth or vicious growls. They don't have quills or jagged claws. But they've got legs. When that fear and instinct kick in, they move. They flee; they leap. And far from being a "sad" response—simply because "flight" animals seem weaker to us than "fight" animals—it's what makes them mighty. Their fearful instinct fuels their nerve.

If we want to get past feeling stuck in life, conquer our fears, and move into the places God calls us to and do the things he asks us to, we need to grab hold of some nerve ourselves. We need to let our fear be not what holds us back, but what triggers a response. To be the thing that lets us call on the Holy Spirit to help us live mightily for God.

If I Only Had the Nerve

Nerve. I've been a big fan of the word ever since I first heard the Cowardly Lion singing out his longing for it in The Wizard of Oz. But honestly, I hadn't given it much thought until a recent e-mail exchange about fear with my friend Tracey, the "I'm not afraid" pastor from the last chapter.

Tracey had been told during her ordination that, while

pastors tend to appear fearless, it's simply because they've "moved to a place of getting over that initial fear."

"Pastors have a lot of nerve," she was told. Tracey has learned that it takes a lot of nerve to dash into an ER and sit by a family experiencing heartbreaking trauma. It takes a lot of nerve to stand up in front of a crowd and talk about God. She says she's scared every time she has to get up and preach, but somehow she finds the nerve.

Though *finds* might be the wrong word. *Calls up* is probably better. While a deer's nerve can be found—since it comes straight out of instinct—the rest of us do better to go someplace else. Or to Someone else, as it may be.

You see, while fear has the power to paralyze us and keep us stuck, it can trigger something else. In deer, it's fear that triggers their instinct, that propels them, that makes their tiny hooves and sinewy legs spring into action. Fear releases them to do their beautiful leapy thing, to showcase what God made them to be.

Fear can propel us to do our own beautiful leapy things, to showcase what God made us to do.

For those of us who seek to follow God, fear can be the thing that propels us, too; that allows us to do our own beautiful leapy things, to showcase what God made *us* to do.

While God speaks in Scripture so often about not being afraid, we aren't just left with that. We get more reassurance. We get:

> *For the LORD your God goes with you; he will never leave you nor forsake you.* (Deuteronomy 31:6, NIV)

We get:

> *Do not be afraid as you go out to fight your enemies today!*
> *Do not lose heart or panic or tremble before them. For*
> *the LORD your God is going with you! He will fight for*
> *you against your enemies, and he will give you victory!*
> (Deuteronomy 20:3-4)

And we get:

> *I will trust in him and not be afraid. The LORD GOD*
> *is my strength and my song; he has given me victory.*
> (Isaiah 12:2)

So much beautiful language surrounds these "Do Not Be Afraid" passages that once you start reading these, you can't get enough. And there are a bazillion of them.* I believe God gives us these words because he doesn't want us simply to stop shaking in our boots when we feel scared, but he asks us to step up, step out, or leap. God calls us to live fully and bravely. He calls us to have nerve.

But of course, it's not nerve of our own power God's looking for. Our fear should always trigger a call to God, seeking his might. And that always—always!—comes from the Holy Spirit.

Spirit-Led Living
My son Henrik recently asked me why we don't celebrate Pentecost. When I balked—and said we do—Henrik said,

---

*See the appendix on page 249 for more of my favorites.

"No. I mean *celebrate* it. With a party. We celebrate Jesus being born, why not the Holy Spirit coming down?"

The kid has a point.

When I shared my son's wisdom with my pastor-friend Gregg, he told me that he thought we didn't celebrate it because the Holy Spirit freaks us out. We don't know what to do with it. Plus, Gregg thought maybe Pentecost falling right between Mother's Day and Memorial Day and all those graduation parties and just before those weddings, well, you know. We get busy.

I think Gregg is right about both these things, but the freaking us out bit makes the most sense. After all, I don't think anybody was carving turkey or singing carols on Pentecost, even before Mother's Day and graduation were commonplace.

The truth is, the Holy Spirit freaks us out. We're okay with the Spirit as a distant gift-giver, or even a quiet indweller. And we're good when we're looking for peace and comfort, maybe a quick word of encouragement. We love those sweet whispers, those gentle passing thoughts that fill us with stillness and ease. But that sweet love-dove of a Holy Ghost doesn't exactly tell the whole story.

Consider what happened on Pentecost. It was crazy. Here's how Luke explains it:

Suddenly, there was a sound from heaven like the roaring of a mighty windstorm, and it filled the house where they were sitting. Then, what looked like flames or tongues of fire appeared and settled on each of them. And everyone present was filled with the Holy Spirit and began speaking in other languages, as the Holy Spirit gave them this ability.

At that time there were devout Jews from every nation living in Jerusalem. When they heard the loud noise, everyone came running, and they were bewildered to hear their own languages being spoken by the believers. (Acts 2:2-6)

These devout Jews who showed up to this scene thought everybody there was drunk. Understandable.

But what amazes me is that when they realized the crazy-talking folks weren't drunk, they wanted in. They wanted what the Holy Spirit was pouring out. The Bible says about three thousand people repented and were baptized that day.

All that tongue-speaking, pseudo-drunken revelry wasn't the end of the madness, either. Those Spirit-filled people continued to do crazy, crazy things, like:

- share everything they had
- sell property and possessions and share the money with those who needed it
- worship at the Temple *every* day
- share meals with "great joy and generosity"

And the best part? While they did this, they praised God and enjoyed "the goodwill of all the people" (Acts 2:47).

Frankly, this is why we freak. Because the Holy Spirit swoops down from heaven with banging and fire, and the holy flames lick our bodies and make us do crazy things: like speak in tongues we've never spoken before and—oh, no!—like share *everything* we've got with other people. And feel great about it!

How many of us read this and pray, "Dear God, please don't make me do that!"

It all seems so scary. And yet, the witnesses—who saw the Holy Spirit at work and alive in people—were drawn to that. They wanted it. They wanted to live it. Because as terrifying as it can seem, being Spirit-filled and Spirit-led is a wonderful, mighty way to live.

I want to have that "Acts 2" deep sense of awe and life change. I want to share my meals with great joy and generosity while praising God and enjoying goodwill. I want to look around at all my stuff and say, "You know what? This is too much!" and sell it and give money to those who need it much more than me.

Beyond that, I want to do what God has gifted me for and what the Holy Spirit is prompting me to do. I want to live the life I was created to live—mightily. Even this can be terrifying and seem crazy to those around us. We can fail or get laughed at. Plus, there's "a force," as Donald Miller writes, "in the world that doesn't want us to live good stories. It doesn't want us to face our issues, to face our fear and bring something beautiful into the world."[17]

As terrifying as it can seem, being Spirit-filled and Spirit-led is a wonderful, mighty way to live.

Have you felt this force? I sure have. This force (a lot of us call this force "Satan") makes us doubt that what we feel is real, that what we heard or how we're gifted is really from God, which tries to keep us from living good stories, as Miller says. But what this is really about is being kept from living mightily—from doing the Kingdom work we were put here to do.

God rolls his eyes at this "force." It's no match for him. And no match for us—if we're willing to call up our nerve by calling on the name of God. We need to invite the Holy Spirit to fire us up, to sizzle our fear with fire, and to set us ablaze so that we can live mightily and do what we're made to do.

But Do I Have to Be on Fire?

You should know, I'm smiling a bit as I write this, picturing the image you must now have of me. One that's probably very different from the truth. Let's just say, I'm not as "fired up" as you might think. In fact, the term brings back some jarring childhood memories.

When my parents were born again in the 1970s, they always talked about and admired "on fire" Christians. These types were always hootin' and hollerin' about Jesus and laying on hands and invoking the Holy Spirit and his healing power. These were the people whose arms were always raised in church. Their prayers were powerful and passionate.

My parents tried to emulate these folks—to make this type of connection with God their own. It never felt like it fit me, even when I was a girl. Still today, if you met me and we had some sort of conversation, you'd never come away from our time describing me as an "on fire" Christian. I mean no offense to the on fire set, but I tend not to express my faith that way (much, at least). It's not the way God made me.

I say all this not to ostracize or break us into needless groups, but because you don't have to be on fire in the way my parents saw it to live a mighty, Spirit-led life. You can; you just don't have to. No matter how you express your faith or how you like to worship or pray or whether you like to sway or clap or dance or stand stick still when you sing doesn't make you any more or less in tune or immune to the power or the sensing of the Holy Spirit. None of us are exempt from following his prompts.

No question, I have felt the Holy Spirit. I have held on, mouth open, as the Spirit's Hurricane Wind swirled through a room of soul-bearing, world-changing women. I have felt the Breeze sift through my heart when I needed calming. And I have felt the Wild Fire roar through my body—burning the chaff and sparking passions and gifts.

I have felt the fear that comes with this. *Oh no. What's gonna happen now?*

But I also know that this is the place where life gets good. To reference Donald Miller once again, he calls these moments "inciting moments"—it's the place in a novel or a movie where the story gets good, where it launches everything that comes next. And, he writes, "The great stories go to those who don't give in to fear."[18]

Love that. Living mightily is about living a great story—not to entertain an audience or readers, but to glorify God. So when you're in this place, when you sense the Spirit urging you, pushing you, shoving or tossing you maybe, toward the work you were meant to do, remember: this place where calling and fear meet is the place where God shines brightest, feels warmest, and stands strongest. This is where miracles happen, where you get to experience God like none other. This is where your story gets good. This is a huge key to learning to love your life. But you gotta step out for it to happen.

Stepping Out

I once did a *lectio divina** where the passage was John 21. Verse 7 stuck with me. It says this: "When Simon Peter heard that it was the Lord, he put on his tunic (for he had stripped for work), jumped into the water, and headed to shore."

Part of the mystery of the *lectio* is uncovering why a particular passage speaks to you (or, *reads* you, in fact). My initial reaction to this verse was simply, *Why would Peter put on his clothes to jump into the water? Everybody knows you want fewer—not more—clothes when swimming.*

But as I meditated and mulled on Peter's foolishness, something else emerged. I remembered what happened the

This place where calling and fear meet is the place where God shines brightest, feels warmest, and stands strongest.

last time Peter got out of a boat to meet Jesus.

You remember?

He walked on the water. Walked. On the water! And here I was thinking *Peter* was stupid. I was the dummy. Who knows why Peter put his coat back on—probably to be respectful to Jesus and because it's gross to eat breakfast almost naked—but the bigger point was: who cares? Peter saw

Jesus and wanted to be near him. And he knew his Jesus to be faithful in stormy waters; he probably figured Jesus would be faithful if a cloak weighed him down. So Peter threw on his coat and jumped in and swam to shore.

Lectio divina literally means "divine reading." It's a method of quiet reading/meditation of the Bible, in which the Holy Spirit is depended upon to offer "illumination" on a text. It may sound weird, but it's wonderful. Lectio "purists" will spend an hour a day in this practice. I do a quick version—and maybe only once a month. Google it for more information on this wonderful spiritual practice.

This is the breakfast during which Jesus asks Peter three times if he loves him. And tells Peter to feed his sheep. But what I love best about this scene is when Jesus says this to Peter:

"When you were young, you were able to do as you liked; you dressed yourself *and went wherever you wanted to go. But when you are old, you will stretch out your hands, and others will dress you and take you where you don't want to go." Jesus said this to let him know by what kind of death he would glorify God. Then Jesus told him, "Follow me."* (John 21:18-19, emphasis mine)

Of all the things you can do by yourself when you're young, I love that Jesus picked getting dressed. Maybe Jesus noticed Peter putting on his cloak too. Maybe Jesus even smiled about this—wondering. Probably he was moved by his faith. Regardless, Jesus was laying out some rough road for Peter. One that was terrifying, frankly. But Jesus called Peter—this man of amazing faith—to follow him. And Peter did.

This last passage wasn't part of my *lectio* experience, but it plays into what I've continued to think about ever since.

For me it was pretty clear that God was using this passage to tell me that I need to stop being afraid, specifically of what others will think, and to follow where God is leading.

At the time I thought it had something to do with my kids' school. And part of me still does, as I continue to wrestle with the best option for my kids (while praising God for the options we have). But since then a new fear I need to conquer has entered in. Granted, it seems downright silly. It's certainly not the same kind of scary that Peter had in front of him or that people around the globe face every day, but this act of following where I may be being called feels scary nevertheless.

A therapist once told me "pain is pain" when I downplayed a hurt; I suppose "fear is fear."

Here's the story: Over the past year, two book editors have told me they'd like to see me write a novel (for what it's worth, one of them told me this while rejecting something else I had written). I resisted this. Historically, no good has come from my attempts to make up stories. In fact, thinking back on a couple of short stories from high school and college (the last time I wrote fiction) still makes me shudder—and not just because one was about a motorcycle-riding ghost named Dimitri.

So when these people said I should consider writing fiction, I blew it off. But then somebody else—a book publisher—asked me if I'd consider trying fiction. He thought I'd "do it well."

All this was out of nowhere, so I started praying about it. Then I entered a season of having to wait on a bunch of writing projects (including this one). The writer in me got antsy, eager—but unable to dig my teeth into something big. Then the Holy Spirit chimed in. It wasn't one big crazy Pentecost clamoring, but it's been pretty persistent. In the whispers. In the windstorms. And even in the fires in my soul.

In my whole life, I've never been one of those writers who claimed to have characters walk into their heads. I've never had stories unfold before me. Yet somehow characters started meandering in, saying, "hey," showing me where they live, telling me what hurts, what they're afraid of. Since back in the days when I *had* to write stories, I always failed under my own efforts. I'm wondering if this is the Holy Spirit as Muse, offering me up some creative writing.

If it is, it scares me for a whole bunch of reasons. But mostly because I fear failure. I fear being laughed at. I fear being told that while maybe I can pull off a decent essay, craft a convincing complaint letter, or maybe even grumble enough about life to fill a book, inventing and creating stories will never be for me. I hate the part of sending a chapter to my agent or to an editor or bringing one to my writers group only to hear back, "You know, this just isn't working."

I'm scared. Plain, old scared. Now, this may sound like a silly thing to fear—especially if God is calling you to something much more physically terrifying. (Although, tell Salman Rushdie that life as a writer isn't physically terrifying.*) Or maybe you're not being called to do something scary but to *live* something scary. Maybe you or a loved one is sick or in pain or dying. Maybe your circumstances are often more than you can bear. Maybe each day is just too terrifying to face.

Goodness knows that people around this globe are called to do things and asked to live lives that drive a hot spear of fear through me. And yet God still says not to be afraid—no matter how big or how small or how seemingly silly what lies in front of us seems to be.

---

*After Rushdie's novel, *The Satanic Verses,* was published in 1988, Iran's Ayatollah Ruhollah Khomeini issued a *fatwâ* against Rushdie, as the book was deemed blasphemous to Islam. The threats on his life forced Rushdie to have police protection and live in secrecy for years.

I think a lot about Jesus' mom, Mary, and her calling. How she as a young girl was called to face humiliation, a pregnancy, and a whole lot of stress and sorrow for the sake of all of us, really. Joseph too. I love what Carolyn Custis James says about him in *Lost Women of the Bible*: that Joseph dropped everything to follow *Mary's* calling. Think about that. It's scary enough for a man in this day and age to give up everything—his career, his reputation, his friends, his family, his home. But when Joseph did it, it would have been scandalous.

I think he had the nerve (ditto for Mary)—and followed her calling mightily because he received these words from an angel:

> *After he had considered this, an angel of the Lord appeared to him in a dream and said, "Joseph son of David, do not be afraid to take Mary home as your wife, because what is conceived in her is from the Holy Spirit."*
> (Matthew 1:20, NIV)

So now I ask you a question that I've been asking myself: What has the Holy Spirit conceived in you? An idea? A passion? A desire? A specific task? What is it that you *don't* need to be afraid of, but are?

I've written two chapters of something that could become a novel. Whether it could be a *good* novel I don't know. But I wrote them in "obedience," I suppose. I stopped when I had to work on this book (which, I don't want to mislead you, is also a terrifying call). I hadn't looked at those chapters in several months—although the characters have kind of kept talking to me, popping into my brain every now and again to let me in on something or to show me something they found.

Well, last week, I opened the chapters and reread them with fear and trepidation. You know what? They weren't bad. They weren't great. Trouble is, now I kind of want to know what happens. I like these characters—the ones I think maybe the Holy Spirit conceived in me. So when I'm done with this project, I think I'll go back, keep writing, and see where it leads.

What has the Holy Spirit conceived in you? An idea? A passion? A desire? A specific task?

Of course, I'll be trying to stave off fear and shun those negative voices that pound in my head all the while. But if I don't write it, I'll always wonder, probably regret not having taken the chance. I won't have lived as good a story, as Donald Miller would say.

It's 2010 as I type this. Check Amazon in a few years. If you see a novel by me, terrific. (Order it!) If not, oh well. Kind of embarrassing because you'll know I "failed," but it doesn't mean I lived any less mightily. Or didn't do what God wanted me to. Or didn't learn something wonderful.

That's part of the mystery of the mighty, Spirit-led life. We aren't guaranteed certain outcomes. We aren't guaranteed earthly success. Called people sometimes fail. But failure in one aspect doesn't have to deplete all the joy that comes from following a Spirit prompt, and it doesn't eradicate the meaning or purpose behind an endeavor. My husband felt called to run for state representative and did. He stepped out and ran a great, honest, hardworking campaign. And he loved it. Even when he lost. The election, at least. Because he came away secure that he had done what God called him to. Even if the result wasn't what Rafi would've hoped. He found joy and purpose in following God.

When we step out—when we move toward the mighty life—the only outcome we're assured of is that God is faithful. That he is just. And that he will be with us. That's why we can step out without fear. That's why we can live mightily for him. That's why we can do what the Holy Spirit has conceived in us.

Into Practice

But as I've written a zillion times before, this is all easier typed than done. I know. Yet inviting the Holy Spirit in, allowing our raised arms to be lightning rods for the Spirit's holy fire, for our forearms to be landing spots for the dove (or goose, if you're Irish) to perch on, is what makes us mighty. We need to pray that the Holy Spirit finds us welcoming vessels, courteous hosts to swirl around in and lead us where we need to go.

When we step out—when we move toward the mighty life— the only outcome we're assured of is that God is faithful.

My kids have a CD they like to listen to called *Dog Train*.[19] The album is filled with great kid rock 'n' roll, dance-around-the-kitchen songs sung by some bands I saw back in college. But there's this one song, "Dragonfire," that makes me wobbly. It's so beautiful. I realize this could sound like giant heresy, but whenever I hear the words about a child who feels small and weak but who can summon his own "dragonfire," I imagine the Holy Spirit at work in me. While what we summon isn't "our own," that image of summoning a fire that—as the song says—"burns so bright" is lovely.

I think we can walk through life mightily when we feel the Spirit burning in us, when we're aware of the fire from the one who refines us, who gets rid of the junk in our lives, and who fuels and empowers us when even a small step seems too terrifying to take.

But this SpiritFire can serve another function: it can help us see—and perhaps be a guide to others—when things get dark. It can light our paths when we're being called to put one foot in front of the other or when we know we need to take a giant leap. And after we do, it's what helps us see God's grace for our lives.

OKAY, GOD:

I can feel it. I know where you want me to go. What you want me to do. But this is a big step! This is a huge leap! I want to follow you here, but I'm scared. Help me to be fearless. Help me to be mighty. Help me to do this because I love you. Take my fear and my trepidation. Make me strong and bold for you. May I listen for the rush of the Holy Spirit with great joy and anticipation!

Anyhow, God, Hallelujah.

Amen.

Getting to Hallelujah
Questions for Reflection and Discussion

1. When was a time in your life that you felt especially mighty?

2. What's going on in your life right now that requires some nerve?

3. Are you more of a "fight" or "flight" animal? How might your own reaction to fear fuel your nerve? How does your reaction impede it?

4. How might your life look different—even "better"— if you lived more mightily?

5. What are some of the things or circumstances in your life that keep you from doing things you feel called to do?

6. How might those things or circumstances be overcome?

CHAPTER 6

LIVE ON THE LOOKOUT

Letting Go of Your Expectations about How God Works

OVER LUNCH at our favorite Vietnamese restaurant, my friend Claire and I once talked about how hard it is to wait on God. How annoying it is when we pray and pray and pray and get nada. Then Claire told me about her friend Kate-Lynn.

Kate-Lynn apparently has a particularly close relationship with Jesus. They're tight. According to Claire, Kate-Lynn will toss an arm over the back of a chair and sort of chat-pray to Jesus as if he's sitting right there. (Well, I guess we Christians believe he *is* sitting right there, but Kate-Lynn seems more aware of that than most of us. Or at least more aware than Claire.) And then, it seems Kate-Lynn gets a word or a sign from him on the matter two beats later. Like Jesus just chimes right into the conversation.

Claire explained how if Kate-Lynn had been there with us, she might have prayed for, say, discernment about when to embark on a new project—to the Jesus sitting there with us. Then she'd likely notice the table tent advertising the day's specials in that next moment (somehow, a sign), and then a neon sign flashing above the table tent would be the exact thing she needed to hear from God. It would help her decide which option was best for her.

But here was the kicker, the real reason Claire told me about her friend Kate-Lynn. Kate-Lynn had just been up from the Ozarks to visit Claire, who lives near me, in Chicago. Since Kate-Lynn loves monarch butterflies, they had planned a trip to Brookfield Zoo, to the special, seasonal butterfly exhibit. Another commitment got in the way, though, so they were unable to go. Kate-Lynn was especially bummed, as she loves monarch butterflies. For whatever reason, they have special significance to her. They're symbolic, I suppose.

Well, wouldn't you know it: the very afternoon that they were supposed to head to the zoo to walk among the butterflies, Kate-Lynn sat glum and blue in Claire's normally butterfly-free backyard with a cup of tea, cooling in its thin bone-china cup, set on a saucer (Claire's a fancy, treat-guests-right kind of hostess), praying that God would "show up." That God would help her through this rough patch that she was walking. That God would bring her peace about some current anxiety she couldn't shake. When she said her "amen" and opened her eyes—you guessed it—a monarch butterfly sat perched, its orange and black stained-glass wings together pointing straight to heaven, on the gilt rim of her teacup. Kate-Lynn gasped, and it fluttered its wings, landing a moment on the saucer before flying off again.

Kate-Lynn's reply? A look heavenward as she followed the

butterfly and a sigh: "Thank you, Jesus." It was a confirmation of what she had just prayed about.

Claire told me all this not to trivialize her friend's faith (which has indeed been stomped on many times by life's ups and downs), but to express Claire's own annoyance with God. Claire wondered why some people seem to get all the goods from God (butterflies, neon signs, etc.), while others of us hear crickets chirping in the background every time we pray. Why some of us feel like God is picking at his fingernails and then when we finally yell loud enough, he squints back down at us every once in a while and goes, "Oh, were you talking to *me*?"

Some of us feel like God is picking at his fingernails and then when we finally yell loud enough, he squints back down at us every once in a while and goes, "Oh, were you talking to me?*"*

So after telling me this story—as we walked back toward our cars, as a train clanked along tracks behind us—Claire said, "I've been praying about [her thing] for years and I get nothing. I just want to know: Where's my stinkin' butterfly?"

I loved that question. And even now, I feel the same hollow ache for her as I did when she asked it. Because I've wondered the same thing so much in my life. Wondered why the Kate-Lynns of the world get their neon signs and butterflies and postcards while some people get more questions. And why Bible folks got angels dropping by to give a heads-up while we just get surprises dropped on us. Why some people get such clarity on the most trivial matters, while others of us have to wrestle and wonder about huge choices. Why God seems to zap in and help some people with unexpected bonuses and bags of groceries and lets some people stay hungry. Why he answers some prayers and why he lets some linger. Why some people get instant relief while others feel as if they're drowning in feelings of fear and loss of control.

It's the absolute pits to feel like God is not at work. With you, at least.

But you know what? I think it's our desperation for butterflies in our lives that makes us rush out and try to grab control of life. To make our own butterflies. To answer our own prayers.

We feel so much less deserted by God when we're plodding away at something on our own. Oswald Chambers says it like this: "It is much easier to do something than to trust in God."[20] Isn't that great—and true? And yet, this is the sort of action that leaves us lingering in our stuckiness, like we talked about a couple of chapters back.

We feel so much less deserted by God when we're plodding away at something on our own.

Claire's butterfly question offers some real relief to this. In fact, what I love most about the butterfly question is that if we ask it enough—and ask it of other people—we start seeing our butterflies. Everywhere.

In fact, to be fair to Claire, her story didn't end here. She later told me how she had relayed our conversation—and her frustration—to her husband, who said, "What do you mean, where are your butterflies?" And he began to point out all the ways and places God had been showing up in her life.

All the opportunities that had come out of nowhere. All the experiences that seemed to land in her lap. All the unexpected blessings and roundabout answers that swarmed her life, that landed on teacup rims.

No, God hadn't fixed everything or made everything crystal clear, but he was there. As her husband listed off all the changes and experiences and blessings Claire had enjoyed over the past several months, she began to see even more. Fluttering all around.

"So," Claire told me later, "maybe those are my butterflies."

Yeah, maybe. Probably. Definitely.

I think God sends each of us "butterflies" all the time, but we're just too busy or distracted or whatever to notice them. We're also too focused on everybody else's answers and blessings to see our own. We want exactly what other people get— i.e., we all want butterflies to arrive in the same way.

Or at least, Claire and I do. Which is crazy—especially for me, since I wrote my first book about our identities and how we need to be loved and valued for the unique people we are. I spent a lot of time in that book (and I still spend a lot of time in my speaking) ranting and raving about how we need to interact with one another as individuals—taking into account our personalities and abilities and talents and hopes and dreams—and not as stereotypes or mass-produced people.

And I say we need to do this because it's what God does. We see it in the Bible and we've experienced it in our lives.

So I say all this and then what do I turn around and do? Expect God to show up for me (with my individual personality and ability and talent and hopes and dreams) just like he does for somebody else. I say, if Kate-Lynn gets a butterfly, then I want a butterfly. But God has never worked like that. I think that's because he loves us too much.

Snow Angel

Back to those Bible folks a minute: think about the ways God showed up to people when he wanted them to change course or when he had a little something to say. Moses got a burning bush. Saul got blinded. Mary and Joseph got nice angels. Jacob got a rough one. Ruth got a wise and desperate mother-in-law. Hagar got God himself. Lots of people got Jesus. Peter got a rooster. And Jesus, of course. We could go on and on.

The point is, some of those Bible people got much clearer messages than others. Some people got comforted into taking their next steps, where God was leading. Some people got kind of shaken into it. Some people (Philip) only got the command to "Go south." Only God knows why. But there's no reason to think or expect that God is not guiding you just because he isn't as clear with you as he seems to be with others. Just because the Kate-Lynns of the world get quick answers and butterflies doesn't mean he's more taken with them. It might just mean that they're more in tune to what God sounds like, looks like, feels like—to them. Maybe they just notice.

There's no reason to think or expect that God is not guiding you just because he isn't as clear with you as he seems to be with others.

Maybe they just understand that God doesn't stamp out responses any more than he stamps out people. He likes unique; he likes special. So when we're asking

God to show up, to guide us, to help us, we need to learn to look for how he does this in our own lives and stop expecting him to Xerox what he does for someone else. He doesn't mass-produce answers to prayer. He customizes. Just for you. Just for me. Just for the way he wants our lives to go down. For the things he created us to do and be.

After working on the last chapter ("Live Mightily"), I tweeted that nothing makes you sound crazier than talking about the Holy Spirit. As I prepare to launch into this next little illustration about God tailor-making answers to prayer, I realize there is indeed something that makes you sound crazier than talking about the Holy Spirit: talking about angels. Especially when you say that you believe an angel once picked you up off the side of a Michigan highway in a whiteout and drove you to get help.

God doesn't stamp out responses any more than he stamps out people.

So, okay. Yes. I believe this. I believe that once while I was driving back home from college during a lake-effect blizzard the likes of which is seen only in the far southwestern "wrist" of Michigan's mitten, an angel in a wood-sided Jeep Wagoneer rescued me after my car spun out and landed in a ditch. I believe this because during the whole stretch of white-knuckled, wheel-grasping driving I did during that storm there was only one car behind me—a mid-1970s pea green something-or-other. Maybe a Chevy Nova, like my grandmother had. Other than the pickup truck whose tracks I steered my own little Volkswagen in, I saw no other cars. Certainly not this Wagoneer.

But after I spun out on that stretch of isolated, wooded

highway, after my car slid down the embankment and into the ditch amid my quick-breathed prayers for help, I looked up and saw the Wagoneer. Right up in front of me, safe and sound on the shoulder.

A woman—probably forty ("old" to my twenty), with a preppy, smooth bob and burgundy lipstick—leaned toward the passenger-side window and waved me over.

When I pushed my door open across heavy snow, she looked behind her—at the green Nova-ish thing with the skinny, bearded man getting out—and said, "Grab your purse and get in now. Leave the rest. Daddy's got insurance."

The weirdness of what she said struck me, and yet the snobby tone of her command and the sight of this small woman—whom I now saw wore a red, leather-collared barn jacket unbuttoned enough to reveal a row of creamy pearls—in a big car made me feel instantly safe. Though she was a stranger, everything about her was familiar.

In a situation where I had few other options, I heeded her advice and got in. She took note of the mile marker nearest my car (something I'd never have thought to do) and drove me a couple of miles to the next exit—near St. Joe's—where she found a service station for me. I didn't have cash to pay the tow truck driver, so she paid him the thirty bucks and gave me a hug good-bye before I got into his truck to take me back to my car.

It was during this ride—with the big strange man, in a big strange truck, curving back north, along that tuck of snow-covered Michigan—that I began to pray again, thanking God for my rescue and asking for safety in this current situation. I had a sense then of God saying, *Would I have saved you then, only to let you die now?* (As I type this today, I think it may echo some Scripture, no?)

That's when that woman became an angel in my head. That's when I realized her Jeep had seemingly come out of nowhere. That's when I realized that the shopping bags in her backseat were from stores (familiar and comforting to me, in my life as it was then) in Chicago. They weren't in Holland— where she said she was coming from.

Granted. I may be wrong. She's probably just flesh and blood and living it up in St. Joseph, Michigan, as we speak. I may be off—and crazy—thinking that she was an angel, sent specially by God. Just for me in my moment of need.

Or maybe she really was an angel who just got mixed up in the props room when she picked up those Marshall Field's bags.

But I'm not off in my thinking that God sent or used this woman to help me—and he used about the only type of person that a twenty-year-old me would not be afraid of.* This perfectly suited hero (whether mortal or ethereal), combined with my God-given good sense, allowed me to be rescued.

If I'd have ignored this, if I had turned off my senses, God knows what would've happened. I still shudder thinking about the lanky green-Nova guy as he stared at us while we pulled away.

I've thought a lot about this day when I'm lost in my pity parties, wondering where God is and why he's not coming when I call. Like when we talked about Peter in the last chapter—who must've remembered his walking on water

---

*Since then, I've seen enough documentaries about the *one woman* who looks so kind and sweet and "wouldn't hurt a fly" and heard about enough crazy suburban moms who killed their own kids to know that not everyone who looks or talks a certain way is safe. But I bet you know what I'm getting at here.

when he put *on* his coat to jump in the water to see Jesus. It reminds me of God's faithfulness and that he takes into account who I am whenever he shows me who he is.

It's pretty cool. He tailor-makes rescues. Of course, contrary to what I may sound like, I'm not a big damsel-in-distress type person. So I want to be clear that when we're looking for our butterflies, it's not all about rescue. It's not all about being saved; sometimes we just want to be *shown* the way. We just want to see. Since he goes through all the trouble to tailor-make all his responses to our prayers, I think God wants us to use our eyes as well.

Here's how I know this.

Open Your Eyes

When I was home from college one summer (probably the summer before my little ride with an angel), I decided to test the whole idea of "walk by faith, not by sight" while bike riding. You probably see where this is going.

I had just taken a nice, long ride by myself along the Prairie Path—a former railroad line that now intersects northern Illinois and carves an alternately lushly wooded and sparse prairie path (hence the name) through my town. During the whole ride I had been thinking about God and his role in my life. Big stuff for a bike ride, but what better time, really.

You should know that during this season of my life, I fought with God a lot. I loved him. Believed in him. But I questioned a lot of what he had to say. Or, at least, what Paul had to say. About women, you know.

But during this bike ride, I wasn't thinking so much about Paul's words on women as much as I was thinking about his words on walking—specifically, his commendation that we "walk by faith, not by sight" (2 Corinthians 5:7, KJV). This really nagged at me. I wanted to know what it meant. What it looked like. How it was lived out.

My genius idea? As soon as I took the narrow dirt trail down off the Prairie Path and got back onto the quiet, house-lined road that led to my parents' house, I decided to put Paul to the test. See if he really knew what he was talking about.

If you should walk by believing and not by seeing then surely you should be able to ride a bike by believing and not seeing. Right, Paul?

Boy, did I prove him wrong. It probably took about five seconds after I closed my eyes and prayed, "Lord, I trust you to guide me," for me to hit the curb and flip right over and off.

While I think God probably did cue an angel (though, sans Wagoneer) to buffer my fall, since I didn't break a bone—most notably my neck—when I flew off my bike, I sort of sensed God sighing as he watched me roll over in the parkway, wiping tears from my cheeks and grass and gravel off my bloody knees.

While some could argue—maybe even Paul—that I crashed because I didn't have enough faith (I'll never try to move a mountain), I think maybe God had another lesson for me. In fact, I'm pretty sure that as I limped back to my bike and lifted it out of the street, I heard him murmuring under his breath, "I meant have faith, not be stupid."

Okay, so I don't really believe God called me stupid, but I do believe he let me learn a lesson the hard way. And I still have the scars on my knees to remind me that believing God and having faith doesn't mean you do dumb things. It doesn't mean you close your eyes while riding a bike. It doesn't mean you court danger for danger's sake. It doesn't mean you shut down your senses—common and otherwise.

You know, now that I've calmed down about Paul, and even understand what he was getting at a bit better (even with women), I'm pretty sure Paul was talking about the way we view eternal things—things we can't use our eyes to see—and not about turning off our senses while still plodding the ground on this side of eternity.*

In fact, I think one of the greatest ways to live our faith, to follow our callings, and to know what God is doing—how he's responding to our cries—is by keeping our eyes open and staying on the lookout for what God is up to. All the while

One of the greatest ways to live our faith is by keeping our eyes open and staying on the lookout for what God is up to.

we should be expecting to see signs of what he's doing in this world—for others and for us. We need to pay attention; we need to notice. Especially in times when we feel like God is oh-so-far-away, we need to be attuned to his leading and his grace. We need to know what the signs of his direction are and what they look like in our own lives. And we need to stay watchful, mindful, sniffing and touching, tasting along the road to know where he wants us to go.

But ach. This question—"where should I go?"—is my most dreaded and most clearly unanswered prayer. Aside from the cries of the sick, lonely, and hungry, I suspect that these desperate cries for direction and guidance are among the most common God hears. They've got to be.

---

*Although Paul did have the chance to walk while blind—physically—and fared better than I.

Asking for Directions

I once had breakfast with a friend and her famous-ish pastor, whom I'll call "Ken." He joked with us that this particular pancake house was packed with pastors praying with people* for "direction" in their lives. Ken said, "I just want to tell them: How about *forward*?"

This made me laugh then and still makes me laugh now. Probably because I had just been praying for direction for another person (though I didn't tell Ken!). Actually, while Ken might scoff, I totally think his joking was God's honest truth—spoken directly to me in that moment.

While certainly there are times we feel overwhelmed by choices or confused by callings and need to pray for some clarity and direction, honestly, it's not like most of us are wrestling with that many choices—good ones, at least. Just like we talked about in chapter 4, when we feel lost or confused or stuck and are frustrated with God for not telling us where to go, often the road and the map are clearer than we think. We're just too scared to go there (i.e., move forward) or too impatient to wait.

But even when God seems to be holding us by the collar, asking us to hold tight a spell, forward is still the direction we need to be thinking. It's the direction God's creation moves—nothing really stands still and nothing really goes backward. Trees, even with their roots sunk deep into the earth and their bodies hard and sure, move forward—through time and space and by reaching, stretching, and bloating ring by ring.

If you stop to think about where God wants you to go,

---

*I hope you enjoy the alliteration. I sure did.

really, forward is the only direction. If he does have you by that collar, you might only be able to take baby steps or go at whatever pace he's going—or you may only move forward in the way you think or feel. But that's the direction we're given here on earth.

Even when God seems to be holding us by the collar, asking us to hold tight a spell, forward is still the direction we need to be thinking.

What forward looks like to each of us is a different story entirely. This is where all of this—all my whacked-out stories in this chapter—starts coming together. We need to not only learn to live led by the Spirit (like we talked about in the last chapter), but by what God has given us and by how he's made us. We need to live on the look-out for God at work in everything, and we need to notice how he shows us things.

As many times in my life as I've felt "clueless" as to where I should go, as to what forward was toward, I've really known all along. I've never known (though I once thought I did—something we'll talk about in the chapter on expectations and lies) where it would land me, but I knew what I was supposed to do.

So do you. If you look deep and get real honest. If you crack open the Bible every now and again and read it. Really read it. And meditate on it.

I think the Parable of the Talents speaks to this beautifully.[21] The gist of it is this: God expects us to take care of what we've been given. God has given me children, so my forward means protecting, loving, nurturing, guiding, and providing for those kids. God has given me talents and abilities. My forward there means using them, crafting them, sharpening them. God has given me resources. My forward there means sharing them. God has given me passions and concerns. My forward there means voicing them, exploring them, pressing for change with them.

When we look at it through this lens, it's really not that difficult to see where God wants us to go in our lives. It's also pretty easy to start seeing avenues in which we can use what God has given us and all the places he's showing up with open arms, hands out, offering us avenues of rescue and purpose and direction. We just have to pay attention. We just have to notice.

I realize this is incredibly annoying to read if you're in a place where you just want something specific. If you feel so lost and over-whelmed and alone that you just want some-one to tell you what to do. Exactly. Precisely. I get that. If God could chime in and type for a second here (and I realize he could; I'm just guessing he won't), he'd tell you that I pray for specifics all the time. All the time!

We need to live on the lookout for God at work in everything, and we need to notice how he shows us things.

If God had a nickel for every time I prayed, "Just tell me which city, God. Tell me what job! Just tell me what to do!" he'd be rich. Just send me a stinkin' butterfly, God.

But I've prayed enough of those prayers to know that we may never get the specific answers we long for. The Kate-Lynns of the world may. The Zechariahs and Elizabeths of the world sure did. (How many people struggling with infertility would love to hear, "Your prayer has been heard. Your wife Elizabeth will bear you a son, and you are to call him John"?[22]) Even SpongeBob gets it in one episode. But most

97

of us don't ever get those sort of clear directives; we never hear those wonderful specifics.

I've learned to be almost (almost!) glad we don't. Because as annoying as it is not to get directions while you're in the midst of things, when you're lost and scared and confused, as soon as you get down the road a bit and have the chance to look back and see where you've been, you can hardly believe what God has been up to. And what's happened to you.

As annoying as it is not to get directions while you're lost and scared and confused, as soon as you get down the road a bit and see where you've been, you can hardly believe what God has been up to.

If you're like me, the more lost and scared and confused you get, the more you seek God, the more you cling to him, the more desperate you are for him. And you know what? God likes that. I'm not saying he likes us miserable and scared (he doesn't want us to fear, remember?), but he likes to be sought. He likes to be clung to. He likes us desperate and needy for his love. For him.

So I think sometimes he keeps us in those waiting or stuck places until we learn to look for him and notice him and what he's done for us. Only then can we feel his hands and smell his Spirit and taste and see that the Lord is indeed good.

Noticing

Here's the truth: God is faithful. God hears our prayers. God says to you and to me all the time, "Your prayer has been heard." But we can't notice the answers to questions we forgot we asked.

So if I can get real practical a minute here: One of the best ways to stay on the lookout for how God is leading you or answering your prayers is by writing down your prayers, your laments, your frustrations, your questions. I hesitate to use the words "prayer journal" because it sounds so quaint and is such a cliché, but I suppose that's what I mean.

As a writer I probably shouldn't admit that I'm a terrible journal-er, but I am. I hate journals. Always have. Anytime somebody tells me to "keep a journal"—or worse, uses *journal* as a verb—I groan. So feel free: groan away.

We can't notice the answers to questions we forgot we asked.

But let me tell you about my idea of a prayer journal. I simply mean: jot down your prayers, your questions, your laments, your annoyances, your frustrations, your confusion. On anything. Index cards, little notebooks, the backside of a grocery list, whatever. Write two words or write five pages. Whatever you need to remember. And then cram all those notes in the same place. A place where you can go back and visit. Where you can look and see what God has done.

Honestly, it's crazy. Especially when you pray the big prayers—the bold prayers. The ones where you tell God you want to follow him. No matter what. The ones where you say you want to be led by the Spirit. To go and do what God would have you do. The ones where you say you want a life free of the expectations of this world and full of the expectations of God. The ones that say you will follow if he shows you where to go.

When we write stuff down and go back and reread it, we start seeing how God answers us, how he talks, how he nudges, how he moves and lights our forward path. Not that he'll always do stuff the same way, but it sure makes us more aware of the ways he does things. When we're aware of what we're asking for, we're more likely to notice the passage of Scripture, the paragraph in the book, the verse in the song, the casual comment from a friend.

We begin to see that God's always got something up his sleeves for our lives. When we revisit our prayers, we see that sometimes God is slow to reveal what he's got working. Sometimes he's very Victorian, just teasing us with a glimpse of his wrist, but sometimes he goes all out, giving us a clear view all the way up to the shoulder. Sometimes it's the armpit, when we have to go through some ick to get where he wants us.

But whatever the answers are—clear or convoluted, fast and easy or hard-won—we need to mark those, too. Write them down. And just keep looking for God. For what he wants us to learn. What he wants us to see or to know. Or even to protect us from.

And then give thanks for all those butterflies. And remember.

OKAY, GOD:

I really would love if you could make yourself a bit more obvious from time to time. To reveal yourself and your will the way you seem to do for others. But since that doesn't seem to be happening, let me notice you. In everything. And let me sense your glory and your goodness and your faithfulness all around. I know you're here. Thank you for being with me, for walking forward with me—even when I don't sense your presence.

Anyhow, God, Hallelujah.

Amen.

Getting to Hallelujah
Questions for Reflection and Discussion

1. How would you describe your relationship with God? Like Kate-Lynn's, full of butterfly moments? Or more like Claire's, just waiting for a word?

2. What are some of the weird, unexpected ways that God has shown up in your life?

3. If forward is the only direction we can go—really—what might that mean for you? What does forward look like in your family? in your job? with your passions? with your talents?

4. Write down some of the areas in your life where you hope to see God work.

PART III

Prefer Your Own Hallelujah

CHAPTER 7

LIVE SATISFIED

Letting Go of Jealousy and Constant Comparison

At the end of a busy and draining meeting of my beloved Redbud Writer's Guild (my writers group), our founding member Shayne suggested we end in prayer. So each of us went around, offering up our prayers for guidance and for wisdom. We asked for blessings and that our work and our words would bless others. We asked for clarity and that our writing would glorify God. We prayed for the right words (always need the right words).

And then Suanne prayed. She asked that God would keep jealousy at bay in our group.

I don't know if I shuddered on the outside, but I sure did inside. While each of us prayed something important—and needed—I think Suanne offered up perhaps the greatest need. At least, concerning our group as a whole.

Here's the deal: this writers group is one of the best things I've got going in my life. I think each of the members would say this. I love these women. I love who they are. I love what they do. I love their passion and their drive and their desire to change this world. And I love supporting them and cheering them on. I will go to bat anytime, anywhere for any of them. But, by golly, we're all writers. And that can be a problem. A big one.

If you don't know any writers, let me clue you in. We are needy, insecure, selfish little beasts. Wonderful, don't get me wrong. But still, as a rule, we have issues.

Beyond that, essentially, we're all competitors. In a world where numbers float between 250,000 and one million for new books published each year, all fighting for shelf space, media attention, and the eyes of overwhelmed readers, this creates competition—even among the best of friends.

So when you've got needy, insecure, selfish little competitive beasts gathered together even in a wonderfully supportive, creative, and positive environment—critiquing work, complaining about editors or agents or entire publishing houses (well, the others may do this—not me, of course), and celebrating successes and loving the whole process—it really creates a situation rife for another needy, insecure, selfish little competitive beast to slither in, holding up a piece of glittering fruit. More often than not that fruit is envy and comparison.

Suanne was right to pray for protection against jealousy, because if anything could tear apart our wonderful group, it would be this. It would be if we let ourselves compare and compete and become envious. And I guarantee that's what the devil is going to be working on.

How easy it would be for Satan to start dropping thoughts into our brains: *How come she got that book deal and not me?* Or, *Why did her book sell so many copies when mine is better—and I really need the money?* Or, *She got invited to speak WHERE?!?!* Or, *Her Amazon rank is WHAT?!?!* How simple it would be for those thoughts to wriggle their way down deep into our brains until something so sweet turns to gall.

Frankly, it happens to the best of us. All the time. It's not just an issue among writers—it's a problem in every kind of community, in every type of relationship. Envy is the thing that kills.

Relishing Jealousy

If you'll indulge me, I'd love to take us back a bit—to me, crying there on the kitchen floor. Back to my dark midafternoon of the soul when I said, "I hate my life." Remember?

While the reasons behind my hatred were deep and painful and real, the trigger for tears, for that meltdown that very day was nothing other than good old-fashioned American envy. I had been over at an acquaintance's immaculate, roomy house. One with a beautiful kitchen—straight out of a magazine. (You may have even seen it in one, because it's used as a set.) As much as I hate to admit this, especially since her home is not one I'd ever choose for myself, the idea that she could walk from one room to another without running into a piece of furniture or tripping over a toy, that she could not only afford granite countertops but could consider replacing them just because she was sick of the color, and that she could have custom curtains made for each window made me jealous.

That she had a party for a group of women who stood around and chatted about getting babysitters so they could shop to fill the time when their husbands were traveling with their high-paying jobs made me jealous.

That her kids played quietly downstairs while we chatted upstairs on catered goodies while my kids clung to me made me jealous.

So that's what happened just before my dark midafternoon.

Looking back, it's ridiculous. Even then, I knew it. I knew better than to do the old "judge another person's outside by your insides"—even at the time. But that's what makes jealousy and comparison so dangerous in our lives. Something about it is actually quite delicious. We learn to relish it. Almost crave it. Satan makes that envy fruit so golden and delicious.

And so, even when we know it makes no sense, even when we know we're not seeing the full story, even when we know those same people are probably jealous of us about something, we chomp down. We suck in the juice. We let envy swirl around in our mouths. We savor comparison and competition as they pass over our tongues. They can taste and feel so good—almost like sweet justice.

Yet once they're in, these evil twins of envy and comparison are tough to digest. They don't go down easy—what starts as sweet nectar on the tongue turns acidic on the way down. And once they're down, they start eating *you*, leaving big, empty holes in your heart, soul, and mind.

Even with all the pain that envy and comparison cause, they're not that easy to get rid of either. They hold on. But you can shake them. If you're willing to do some work.

Something about jealousy is actually quite delicious. We learn to relish it. Almost crave it. Satan makes that envy fruit so golden and delicious.

Spitting Out Envy

I wish we could permanently end jealousy and comparison, but since our faith tradition entails us recognizing our fallenness and brokenness and continued need for God's grace, I don't think we can, actually, get rid of it on this side of heaven. But what we can do is become so hyperaware of the dangers of jealousy and comparison and become so vigilant in keeping them out of our systems that we develop a pretty good gag reflex—we learn to spit them right back out as soon as they come in.

My ridiculously in-shape neighbor (I'm jealous of her abs, for what it's worth) once spit out a cookie at a block party because it was "not worth the calories." I watched her in amazement and moderate horror because to a cookie lover like myself, there's not a cookie on earth that's not worth the calories. However, the image sunk right in. It's what I picture myself doing every time I'm tempted to indulge in some jealousy or every time I get a taste of comparison. I remember it's not worth it and spit it out.

Of course, had I paid better attention to what God's Word says about envy, I'd have saved myself some trouble. According to Scripture, jealousy kills us, is stupid (like chasing the wind), and is one of the big sins that defiles us. Check it out:

Surely resentment destroys the fool, and jealousy kills the simple. (Job 5:2)

I observed that most people are motivated to success because they envy their neighbors. But this, too, is meaningless—like chasing the wind. (Ecclesiastes 4:4)

It is what comes from inside that defiles you. For from within, out of a person's heart, come evil thoughts, sexual immorality, theft, murder, adultery, greed, wickedness, deceit, lustful desires, envy, slander, pride, and foolishness. All these vile things come from within; they are what defile you. (Mark 7:20-23)

All this to say, don't just take it from me. God thinks you ought to spit out jealousy and gag on comparisons too. Like I said, I haven't gotten this down to a science, but here's where I started. If you struggle with this, it can help you too.

Taking Inventory

A couple of years back, Carla Barnhill, with whom I founded our *The Mommy Revolution* blog (a site devoted to exposing all the silly expectations put on "good Christian mothers"), wrote a post called "Carla Is Jealous of Your Facebook Status." It was one of our most-read posts ever. I think it has gotten more comments than any other.

In that post, Carla copped to being jealous of the things people said they were doing, like having a house to themselves, getting the best Valentine's Day gift. Whatever.

After admitting her former jealousy of people in Pottery Barn catalogs, Carla writes, "It was one thing when those 'other people' were abstract homeowners in the decorating porn magazines and catalogs. Now, they are real people who remind me of their fine and happy lives via their Facebook updates. . . . I know it's so petty. I know. But we're being vulnerable here and the truth is that there are times when the goodness of someone else's life hits the little places of disappointment in my own."[23]

I followed up on her post with my own crazy admissions. I wrote:

> THIS is a huge problem area for me. I know I have a problem because I was once jealous of a 55-year-old male colleague's FB update that said he was "sitting on his back deck, with a glass of wine, eating roast duck." Last week, I was jealous of a friend who was eating "steel-cut oatmeal."
>
> Mind you: I hate duck and I don't even know what steel-cut oatmeal is—or why or if it's any different than the regular Quaker. But I was JEALOUS of the fact that . . . these people were—at the time—seeming to enjoy a quiet meal and some simple peace. Both of which are "losses" of mine, as Carla wrote about.
>
> I am, of course, also jealous of anyone who writes about going to their cabin (Carla!) or reading quietly next to a fire in Door County (Melinda!) or heading to some sunny, warm place (half the friends I have!). Again, this taps into something I deeply long for.[24]

Making a List, Checking It Twice

Writing that post on Facebook statuses helped me take an important step in my battle with envy. Even though I didn't list everything I'm jealous of in the post, it did make me take inventory of the bazillion things of which I am actually jealous. You can't get rid of what you don't know is there, right?

So, I made a list. And I've kept making lists—whenever I

get a whiff of envy, whenever I sense it lurking. It's the only way I know what I need to get rid of.

Just the other day—in preparation for this chapter—I plunked down at my kitchen table, where I could see my kids swing and chase each other in the backyard, and wrote a list of the things I was jealous of. Here's what was on my list.

I am jealous of people with:

- lake houses
- converted barns to write in
- horses
- parents who are still married
- free time
- sabbaticals from work
- kids in school all day
- enough money to give to lots of organizations
- the ability to write a page-turning novel
- success[*] as writers
- flat stomachs
- time and money to go shopping downtown

And I ended it with "neat freaks." There. I am also jealous of neat freaks. But that made me think of college for some reason, so I added "college students." I am jealous of college students because it's such a great stage of life.

So it wouldn't be all about me and my crazy jealousies, I put out a request on Facebook to see what my friends were jealous of right at that moment. Here's what I found out:

---

[*] And here, by success, I do mean writers who make tons of money. Sorry.

Denise is jealous of people who look good without having
to brush their hair.

Kim is jealous of Denise.

One Bonnie is jealous of other people getting respect or
attention from someone she loves—when they're not
giving it to her.

Another Bonnie is jealous of people with the same gifts as
her. (I assume she means when that person gets more
respect or attention from it—like the first Bonnie said.)

Kathy agrees with the second Bonnie.

Halee is jealous of people who have finished their
dissertations.

What I love about asking other people what they're jealous of is that it helps me see how silly envy is. For example,
I know what Denise's hair looks like and can't imagine why
she'd be jealous of anybody else's. I think I know what gift
both the second Bonnie and Kathy have that
they're probably jealous of in others—both
of them have amazing (but different) voices
that 99.9 percent of the rest of the planet
would be jealous of.

*What I love
about asking
other people
what they're
jealous of is that
it helps me see
how silly envy is.*

But, to be honest, Halee's and the first
Bonnie's confessions do make some sense
to me (so does the gift one, actually, per
my writers group comments earlier). I
get that.

So it seems to me we've got a couple of choices to
make when it comes to jealousy. Assuming we don't want
to stay jealous, we can (a) change our situation to obtain

what we're jealous of or (b) we can lay it down or lift it up (whichever image works best). In other words, we can give it to God.

Let's go back to my list. Take my jealousy of people with flat stomachs. I could probably change this. I'm a naturally thin person; it probably wouldn't be too hard to flatten my tummy. So what should I do? Run every day? Do sit-ups? Spit out cookies? That would probably do it.

Here's the problem: just typing those words made me nuts. I hate running. Bleh to sit-ups. And you already know how I feel about spitting out cookies. And since I'm not a fan of plastic surgery, if I'm not going to change the circumstance— or for other things on my list, if I just can't!—it seems I need to go to option B. I need to give it to God.

At my church, we sometimes pray an Open Hand Prayer, which is where you start by sort of thinking of what needs prayer and pretend to grasp it in your fists. Then you open your hands, palms up, and offer it to God. The last step is to raise your hands up and release it to God.

My friend Suanne says she thinks jealousy is really about our insecurities—and in many ways I think she's right. So, more often than not, in the Open Hand Prayer what we're really releasing is our insecurity or our fear or our worry.

Jealousy is really about our insecurities.

So I do prayer this way all the time with my little envies. You can elaborate on the prayer. Since I'm snacking as I type and can't stop thinking about my stomach (seriously, it's not that bad), I realize I need to release it now. Here's what I'm praying:

God, you gave me three healthy, wonderful children. Each of them grew big (big, big) inside of me and stretched my tummy like crazy, leaving a little extra cushion behind. I know other people have three kids and their tummies seem to zap right back, but thank you for my tummy—the one that nourished and protected my kids. I give you my jealousy. Forgive me for being focused on the wrong things and for being ungrateful. Please take this envy and turn it into something better.

In spite of all the prayers God hasn't answered in my life, when I pray about taking my jealousy, he's all Johnny-on-the-spot. I'm not saying the jealousy doesn't pop back up (a lot of the things on my list have come and gone over the years), but he's good about helping me get rid of envy.

My favorite example of this came several summers ago when I prayed hard for two things: (1) friends who understood my crazy work-at-home mom life and (2) help with my jealousy. God did a two-fer when he answered this prayer by sending me Shayne.

Now, if you're praying for friends, Shayne's a good answer. She's fun, nice, welcoming, passionate, and smart. All the things you'd like in a person. But if you're jealous of the things I'm jealous of—and you're looking for help? Well, she wouldn't have been my first choice.

I'll never forget the day—just after she and I had met for coffee, at the urging of a mutual friend—that I first noticed the pictures on Facebook. Of her cabin. On a lake. In the

Northwoods. Of her kids jumping off a swim platform. Of the new boat her husband bought her.

You need to understand: each of these scenes is pure heaven in my head. It's close to what I once had in my life—and what I now miss. Her real pictures were the ones I longed for in my life. The jealousy that arose was a real, deep kind. This longing ended up being something I needed to grieve (if you skipped chapter 2, you'll need to go back and read it to understand).

I remember looking at those pictures and thinking, *Well, I guess I won't be able to be her friend anymore. That's too bad. I like her.*

As long as I stay aware, envy is replaced by something new and wonderful. Something that adds to my life—that swells my soul, heals my heart, and sends cheers to my brain.

I couldn't imagine what God was thinking. How he could bring someone like *Shayne* into my life when he knew where I was? Knowing our dire financial situation, the wreck of my family life, how could he give me *Shayne* with her happy family photos and a life that seemed free of any financial worries? Clearly, God made a mistake. What does he know anyway?

But then she e-mailed me to see if I'd be interested in being in a writers group with her and—ach—that just sounded so good, so I said, "Yes." And then she just kept being nice and fun and smart and a world changer and all the things I realized I really like in a person. And so because of Shayne I got in this group full of all sorts of wonderful women who understand my crazy life as a write-at-home mom. Women who share that life, even.

And as God answered the one prayer for friends, he also answered the other one. I had to keep releasing and rereleasing some of my Shayne jealousies, but along the way, something weird happened: the envy seemed to evaporate. I still see those pictures—including new ones. I still hear the good things happening in her life, but as long as I stay aware, envy is replaced by something new and wonderful. Something that adds to my life—that swells my soul, heals my heart, and sends cheers to my brain.

That *something* I've discovered is gladness. My new favorite thing. The cure-all for jealousy. (Jealous?) Let's talk about how to get you some gladness in the next chapter.

OKAY, GOD:

So I'm jealous. I wish all sorts of things that aren't mine were mine. I want my life to be like the lives I see around me. And I'm having a hard time being happy for my friends and family who seem to enjoy the things I long for. I need help. I know you've given me so much, so help me appreciate it. Help me be grateful for what I have and help me long only for the things you want to be a part of my life. And please help me never forget the priceless treasure I have in you—my Joy, my Comforter, my Redeemer.

Anyhow, God, Hallelujah.

Amen.

Getting to Hallelujah

Questions for Reflection and Discussion

1. Who or what are you jealous of?

2. How "rational" are these jealousies?

3. Which things or circumstances can you change? Which do you need to turn over to God?

4. Some of the things or people you're jealous of might be pointing you toward something. Can you think of what that "something" is?

CHAPTER 8

LIVE GLADLY

Letting Go of Competition and the Never-Ending Quest for More

YEARS AGO, I was hired to ghostwrite a book based on the Good Sense Budget Course out of Willow Creek Community Church. I have to tell you, working on the project stopped me dead in my greedy, materialistic tracks and spun me right around. No kidding, the job changed my life. So much so that even when I got *fired* from the project, I held no resentment or bitterness. I wished them well—and remain friendly with the people I worked with. I was even *sad* (as opposed to the normal, heh-heh vengeful glee I'm known to spout) to discover later on that the writer hired after me didn't work out either—and that the book idea (at least in that format) fizzled.

All this, because the job had shown me what it looks like to live, what I call, gladly.

I love the word *glad* because it shines in that spot between *happy* and *content.* It's not silly-giddy happy; it's not martyr-ish contentment. *Glad* is a smile and a thankful heart for your life. But I digress. Back to that job in a minute.

While I learned lots on the project—got to talk with fascinating people, hear wonderful stories, pore over wonderful books, and skim catchy and beautiful quotes—it was one little sentence, one simple idea from Dick Towner—the heart, mind, and soul behind the project—that changed me. It was:

"Drive your stake, lifestyle-wise."

"Drive your stake, lifestyle-wise."

—Dick Towner

According to Dick, this means "that there will be a point in time when you declare, 'Enough is enough.' You distinguish between your needs and your wants, between your TRUE needs and what the culture says you need."[25]

Because this idea runs so counter to everything our culture tells us, I'm not even ashamed to admit that the idea of looking around at all I had and declaring it "enough" was an entirely new concept to me at thirty years old. It not only ran against, it shredded to bits everything I had ever learned about what working hard and striving meant.

I grew up an upper-middle class, suburban, private-school Christian. My grandparents were immigrants, and I married a first-generation American. My life was all about the American dream. And to me, the American dream meant that more of everything was better.

Ironically, it's even the reason I took that ghostwriting job. That job paid pretty well. Two big checks gave me as much as I made my entire first year out of college (to date, they're still two of the biggest checks I've ever seen—at least, with my name on them) and would give me more of everything.

But as I pored over the workbook that served as an outline for the book, these words not only started the pounding of the stake into my lifestyle, they pounded a stake almost right through my heart.* They changed me. Even made me a little crazy.

To me, the American dream meant that more of everything was better.

Case in point: Dick Towner suggests that those of us who struggle with competition and "keeping up with the Joneses" go outside and declare our neighbors the "winners" of the stuff wars. I thought it couldn't hurt to try. So, one night when I was feeling overwhelmed with our financial woes and subsequently jealous of a beautiful new home going up down the street, I stood on my porch and said—as Dick suggests—"I give up. You all win. I'm done with this competition."

I'd like to say I shouted this, but I'm not that brave. I'm not convinced that looking completely crazy needs to be a part of this. But if you want to shout it, go for it!

The point is this: declaring others the winners of this silly "keeping up with the Joneses" thing was one of the most freeing acts of my life. That said, I applied it only to the material areas of my life. While it kept me from sliding into crazy jealousy (mostly, anyway) over what money can buy, I continued to slip and screech my way down hills of jealousy toward other things. While it helped curb my jealousy for the *stuff* of life—the furniture, the jewelry, the books, the summer homes, the clothes—I was just as greedy for the *ideas* and *places*.

---

*Yes, this is indeed my "stab" at capitalizing on the vampire craze.

Prefer the Given

My husband will back me up on this: I cannot travel any-where—anywhere!—without going through a whole "I wish I lived here" drill. And it's not just places that are nicer than

Declaring others the winners of this silly "keeping up with the Joneses" thing was one of the most freeing acts of my life.

where I live. Frankly, I live in a nice place. A lovely suburb, minutes (as long as there's no traffic, which there almost always is) from Chicago—one of the greatest cities on the planet. While those of you who live on coasts or near mountains or New York City or some such place may disagree, my neck of the woods—er, prairie—offers some real perks. Sure, we're not zoned for horses or sheep, but other than that, anyone would do well to live here.

And yet, I've been to all sorts of places around this globe and have wanted to live in almost all of them. Some are obvious—Stockholm, for instance (obvious, at least in the summer). Many are not so. Take one of my favorite places, Manitowoc, Wisconsin (again, at least in the summer). Though I cannot figure out an actual reason—like jobs—to move us two hundred miles north, up the Lake Michigan shoreline, every time I've ever driven through this town on our way to one of the other places I'd love to live—Ephraim, Wisconsin—I actually *ache* to move to Manitowoc. Not because it is better than or an upwardly mobile move from where I live (it is, in fact, much cheaper).*

I long to live there because I imagine that living in

---

*I know because I just spent twenty minutes searching property up there to avoid writing. . . .

Manitowoc would make us (or at least, me) happier. That our lives would be simpler, nicer. It ties into another thing I do, which is to believe that if we moved somewhere—to a farm or to the city or by a small town on a lake—that we would be different, that we would become the sort of family who did the things that I imagine make people more satisfied with life.

Of course, this is all bunk—and I've always known it. But it took a simple phrase from my friend Jen to help me with this. I don't remember the conversation we had that led her to share these words with me, but if "drive your stake" was part one of my conversion to the Glad Life, her words to me were part two.

"Prefer the given" is what Jen said. She didn't remember where she heard this,[26] but it had changed her perspective on where she was in life. Even in the most difficult times. Especially in the most difficult times. Jen told me this, in fact, not long after her long-lost sister had come home . . . to die. A time, obviously, of blinding hurt and probable regret over the way life had borne out.

Perhaps it was because this hurt of hers colored the back-drop of her words that they seemed to glisten in the air as she spoke them. These words stunned me with their beauty. And then began to shake me with their power.

I'm always loathe to admit when it's not the words of Jesus—as quoted in Scripture—that rock my world and change my life, but if ever there was a Spirit-infused truth, "Prefer the given" is one.

I just find this so radical and wonderful. One blogger elab-orated on "prefer the given" as this: "Trust that what *is* also *belongs*."[27] Not as succinct, but lovely too, I think, because it allows us to live much more freely and fully in God's will for us. It's the leap of faith that allows us to acknowledge that God's hand is at work and that whatever is going on in our lives is of use to him.

So what does this mean for living gladly? Well, imagine if you could see the circumstances of your life as preferable to something else. Imagine if you could say: I prefer that we've had these money problems or I prefer that I'm battling this illness.

I don't think, actually, that it means that you'd rather be hungry than full or that you'd rather be sick than healthy, but that you prefer the life that God has given you to one you weren't meant to live.

I'd never suggest that someone say "I prefer that I lost my child" or "I prefer that I watch a loved one suffer" but that we, again, prefer where God has put us, the life we are in. That we prefer the grace and strength he offers us even in the most dire circumstances to a life void of his presence and peace. And that we prefer the dark places with God rather than the sun-shiny ones without him.

Prefer the grace and strength he offers us even in the most dire circumstances to a life void of his presence and peace.

But still, this can be hard to digest. And nearly impossible to say. Especially when you're in the midst of dark times. Just as it would be unbearable to utter the words of preferring the loss of a child, so it can be difficult to say that I prefer that my family is in chaos, that I prefer being in debt, that I prefer that my parents are divorced.

And yet, I almost have to if I am to seek to live a life ordained by God, or one that he would have me live. I have to prefer wherever I am, wherever he's put me, whatever he's allowed, or wherever I'm called, and I have to "be thankful in all circumstances" (1 Thessalonians 5:18) if I am to turn the horrors into glory. Or at least, make them manageable.

And now, a word from the devil's advocate who, handily, always seems to pop up her hand even as I type. Obviously, "prefer the given" cannot apply to our own sinful choices— they aren't *given*, after all (though free will certainly is). We cannot prefer a current state of addiction or codependency, say, to one of recovery or boundaries. We cannot prefer a life of crime or purposeful overspending to one of obedience and stewardship.

We are, after all, talking about preferring what we've been given by God (although this is something I try to instill in my kids when it comes to gifts from others as well!), not preferring what we've done.

But then again, even in the midst of our own worst choices and while battling the most tenacious demons, there stands a God ready to give the biggest gift of all—grace. And that's a given we can always prefer.

Into the Confessional

So with those two ideas—driving your stake and preferring the given—fueling our desire to live gladly, we have to look at how this is lived out. Because, let's be honest: we can *be glad* for our own homebound, at-the-community-pool summer all we want until we see that one little picture of someone's perfect cabin, glistening lake, stretching pines, and smiling, wakeboarding family on Facebook. And our gladness goes to pot. And we can *be glad* for our parents—even if they are divorced—until we read stories of someone's grandparents' sixtieth anniversary party and the "legacy of faith and marriage" they gave their kids. And our gladness goes to pot.

If we let it.

In our conversation about jealousy, my friend Suanne offered up a great antidote to envy: confess it. In her case, that meant confessing to a friend her jealousy over an opportunity this person had that she didn't. That act, Suanne says, "was a real growing aspect of our friendship. It's actually made me see how *love* surpasses jealousy in the context of true friendship/relationship and how confessing that burden (for me) was the only way to propel me to an authentic place of encouragement for someone I love and believe in so much."

After acknowledging the disappointment and discouragement she was walking through right then, Suanne continued: "I have had a mirror held up to my face, seeing a lot of ugly and a lot of brokenness in myself that has made life way less about me and my agenda than normal. Seeing my own brokenness has actually been a good 'cure' for my jealousy. For now, anyway. Not totally confident it will last."

And she ended with a smiley emoticon. Her honesty is one of the many reasons I love her.

Along with showing how confession and love can overcome jealousy, she's tapped into something powerful when it comes to living gladly. If we're going to be glad about our own lives, our love for others needs to allow us to feel *glad* for them in their good circumstances. Beyond that, we need to be vigilant about keeping track of our own ugliness—jealous thoughts, vengeful ideas—that keeps us zeroed in on what we want instead of what God wants from our lives.

So, for example, my friend Stacey was over two months ago for tea and snacks when she announced she was heading to France for two weeks by herself. Let me repeat: Heading to France. For two weeks. By herself.

Honestly, nothing could've sounded better to me at that moment. A moment where it was all I could do not to scream and throw something at the wall behind which my kids fought and yelled and the TV blared in the other room. A moment where my conversation with Stacey was weighed down by a sense of how far behind I was (on writing this book) and how overwhelmed I was with work left to do for my "day" job. A moment when I felt like two weeks alone—in France or, for that matter, on the moon—would be the cure for all that ailed me.

So I faced down a choice: Either I could prefer the given in my own life (the noise, the deadlines, and the pressure) and be glad for Stacey. Or I could prefer the gift Stacey got (the adventure, the food, the time to think and write) and seethe with hatred for Stacey and wallow in bitterness for my own life.

Really. That's what it always comes down to. That's our choice.

I went ahead and chose the former. With this choice, I was not only able to stay friends with Stacey, but I was able to truly enjoy her beautiful photos and rejoice with her as I read her posts of her days in Paris and in the south of France.

I still think her trip sounds great—and I do long for some of the scenic peace in which she was able to soul search and pray about where God wanted her and what he wanted her to do—but it's not an opportunity God has given me.

Apparently he wants me to soul-search and pray in a

different kind of peace. Maybe the sort my friend Emily described in a recent tweet: "Something I'm learning . . . gratitude and peace of mind are inseparable." Emily is a songwriter, so she's always tweeting lovely thoughts. But this one particularly struck me.

So much of the frustration I feel in life, so much of why I feel like life has taken a wrong turn or was just not supposed to be this way stems from not having peace of mind.

I have chaos of mind, most of the time. Peace proves increasingly hard to come by. Even on those afternoons when I get to rock on my front porch or stroll through my neighborhood, peace is too fleeting to snatch and reserve for later.

And yet sadly, Emily's tweet touches on something I hadn't considered. Peace of mind doesn't come from outward circumstances. It comes from inside—from just twelve or so inches below that mind. From our hearts. Specifically, from where our hearts feel glad and content.

Peace of mind doesn't come from outward circumstances. It comes from our hearts.

Emily's connecting peace of mind and contentment is brilliant. Probably biblical, even. And it's exactly what living gladly enables us to do. We can live at peace with who God made us and where God put us. When we're content and when we're at peace with this we can, like Paul says, "do everything through Christ, who gives me strength" (Philippians 4:13).

And God not only has a lot of strength to give us, but much more. So instead of looking around at whatever someone else has, let's take a look at what we've got. What God has given us—our things, our circumstances, our location, our friends, our family, our jobs. Look at the good—and the bad—through grateful eyes, and seek the peace that comes with that.

This means that instead of grumbling about bad times and wrong turns, we thank God for them. That we stop striving for *more*. That we *prefer* our circumstances. That we are glad for them. For unpaid bills. For misbehaving kids. For disappointing friends. For unsatisfying spouses. For boring lives. For illness. For confusion. For sorrow. For loneliness.

In the midst of our being glad for things that hurt or frustrate us, we can—and should—certainly still pray for a change in circumstances. Even Jesus did this! But we recognize that God can use all this for the better. For the best! And we live gladly because of it.

OKAY, GOD:

I'm tired of always striving for more and better. I know that this never-ending drive to "keep up with the Joneses" and to meet all expectations is battering my soul. It's keeping me from loving my life and from being thankful for all the things you've given me. Help me be glad. Help me stop the competition. Help me realize that with you, I've already won.

Anyhow, God, Hallelujah.

Amen.

Getting to Hallelujah
Questions for Reflection and Discussion

1. What does the word *glad* mean to you? Does it seem easier or harder to be glad than to be content? How does gladness compare with happiness?

2. What do you have to be glad about right now?

3. What do you miss feeling glad about? How could you find a way to reclaim that gladness even in different circumstances?

4. What might a change of heart, as opposed to a change of situation, do to your feelings of contentment, happiness, and gladness?

CHAPTER 9

LIVE MERCY

Letting Go of Judgment

When my mom called to see if she could take me out for dinner a while back, she caught me in a bad moment. You might have noticed by now that I have a lot of bad moments. It's true. A lot of stress breeds a lot of bad moments.

So, when she asked if we could have dinner, I said, "Ugh. No. Try me again in four weeks."

"Four weeks?" she asked, followed by that *noise* she makes.

"Right," I said, maybe even followed by that noise *I* make. "In four weeks, I'll be done with my book and I'll have time. I can't do it now."

"Okay," she said. Again with the noise.

Now, my mom's response probably would have sounded reasonable to anyone else hearing it. That noise might have even gone undetected. But, alas, I heard her answers with my daughter ears. You know, the ones that funnel every single word through every single annoyance and fight you've had with your mom over thirty-seven years? The ones that can pick up every little *noise*, every little breath, and know exactly what they mean? Yeah, those daughter ears.

The truth is that her *noise* and the *tone* of her "okay" were all that I heard. I knew she didn't believe I was too busy. ("Everybody's busy," she's told me more times than I can count.) I pressed her on it. This started her admission that well, yes, she did wonder how I had so much time to be on Facebook (of all things!) but not for dinner with her.

Mercilessness is my default position when my life gets stressful or when I'm overwhelmed by jealousy or worry or any of the things that make me hate my life.

Then I lost it. Lost it! I yelled at my mother right into the phone. That's right, yelled. At my mother. Into the phone. Because of Facebook.

While I may have had some legitimate reason for being annoyed with her, it would've been reasonable to *explain* the role of Facebook in my life. (Clearly, it's for *work*. It's *research*. You've noticed all the status updates and tweets I quote, right?)

But no matter how many good reasons I had for being annoyed, I had no excuse to yell or to act the way I did. I was horrible to her. I was merciless—yet again.

As much as I hate to admit it, mercilessness is my default position when my life gets stressful or when I'm overwhelmed by jealousy or worry or any of the things that make me hate my life. I start lashing out—either in my thoughts or my actions or my words. And every time I do, every time I don't choose mercy, I get further from the place of love I need to be—for my own life and for others.

Love-Mercy

When my mom and I got off the phone (I actually hung up on her to keep myself from yelling more), I could almost see the shreds of the Fifth Commandment lying beneath me. I had ripped and trampled "honor your mother" under my summer-bare feet.

But it wasn't the worst commandment that I broke in that moment. My words and my tone decimated the one equal to the "greatest" commandment (therefore also making it greatest, which has always tripped me up, but I digress). You know the one: where Jesus is asked which commandment is the most important and he says, "'You must love the LORD your God with all your heart, all your soul, and all your mind.' This is the first and greatest commandment. A second is equally important: 'Love your neighbor as yourself.' The entire law and all the demands of the prophets are based on these two commandments" (Matthew 22:37-40).

That one? Where Jesus says we ought to be loving God with all we've got and then loving others as much as we love *ourselves*? Right. Well, I slaughtered it. And I do it all the time. Any and every time, actually, that I live or act or think without mercy.

Mercy is, after all, one of the great calls of Scripture. I know this full well; it's been kneaded into my conscience since childhood. When I was a girl, I attended Busy Bees, a sort of Girl Scouts knock-off that the Christian Reformed Church did in the 1970s and '80s. While I never quite gelled with this program (it was too craft-centric even for eight-year-old me), the best thing they did for us Busy Bees was to pick Micah 6:8 (NIV) as our theme verse. Every week, we'd recite: "And what does the LORD require of you? To act justly and to love mercy and to walk humbly with your God."

It's still one of the few verses I can recite from memory. It's a good one to have stuck in my head. But while I fear that this verse was chosen because loving mercy and walking humbly seem like simple things for nice little Christian girls to do (our boy counterparts memorized John 14:15—which is all about obedience), this verse packs a serious punch.

It's one of the best "how to live" verses in the Bible—especially when you overlay it with Jesus' words about loving God and our neighbors. So you would think I'd ignore it less. You'd think it would be easier for me to remember to live this out.

If I may take some of the burden off myself, however, I know I'm not alone—because I see it happening, this merciless living, all over the place. I see friends and family, church members and neighbors, loved ones and strangers acting and living without mercy all the time. And most of us never even realize what we're doing.

In fact, many of us think of ourselves as merciful because we *feel* bad for suffering people around the globe; maybe we write an extra check or help out at the local soup kitchen. Maybe we think we're all about mercy because we don't chew out the incompetent waiter who messed up our order—again.

Those are all good, but living mercy encompasses much more when we base it on this commandment to love our neighbors as ourselves. It widens the spectrum, stretching it until it good-aches. In the last chapter we talked about how love enables us to be glad for others (and ourselves). It's the same way with mercy. Love enables mercy. And mercy enables change in the lives of everyone around us (not to mention our own). So we have to learn to live it.

A Mercy Filter

A whole mess of words have been spoken and written on what *mercy* is. No doubt you have a good grip on it. Officially, it can mean a few things, but we tend to think of it in two main ways. The first: "compassion or forbearance shown especially to an offender or to one subject to one's power." The second: "compassionate treatment of those in distress."[28]

And we get this. The first is the sort we show to the incompetent waiter, right? The second kicks in when we cut a check or ladle up soup. Both are the sort of mercy we're pretty good at—or at least that we feel bad about when we aren't.

Yet I worry that these sorts of definitions narrow the scope too much—at least for those of us seeking to follow Jesus and the ways *he* showed and lived mercy. My friend Mike offers something broader and better: "There's always more to the story." When he posted these words, his intention wasn't to redefine *mercy*. I don't remember the context or where he even wrote this—probably on Facebook or on his blog—but because Mike tends to be a merciful sort of guy, my brain applied his words to mercy. I've made what he said my "mercy filter."

While at face value this is a no-duh—not exactly earth-shattering stuff—when you start running circumstances or people or tones of voice through this, opportunities to extend mercy start popping up everywhere.

So, when my mom calls for dinner and I interpret a tone based on my daughter-ears, we get disaster. But what if I had run her tone through my mercy filter? What "more to the story" would I see? Probably a woman who loves me, who's simply disappointed she can't spend time with her daughter, who misses me. I'm a mom. I get that. I doubt very much I would have yelled at that woman. No matter how stressed or tired I was. I'm not an animal, after all. I'd have expressed my love and shown mercy.

When we seek out the more-to-the-story that lies behind every person and every circumstance, we enter into a whole new world. We begin to see things in whole new ways. We begin to see situations and people the way *Jesus* does. Or the way he sure seemed to when he said "hey" to Zacchaeus up in that tree or sat down for a drink next to the woman at the well.*

This idea of seeing things as Jesus does isn't a new concept; you've probably heard it before. Some people have gimmicky names for it like "Jesus Vision" or "Spirit Sight" or something, but I'm not sure it needs a gimmick—just a good effort and a lot of prayer.

Seeing Bull for What It Is

Last winter, my friend Judy chronicled the misadventures of a bull who had wandered away from his farm and into the Orlando subdivision where Judy lives. Apparently, it was fun at first for the neighbors. A little excitement and something to talk about. But as the days dragged on and they could neither "catch" the bull nor find what farm he came from, neighbors started turning on the animal.

---

*I write about Jesus with Zacchaeus and the woman at the well a lot. That's not because I don't know any other stories, but because these are a couple of my favorites. They make me smile and love Jesus more every time I read, think, or write about them. You can read them for yourself in Luke 19 and John 4.

Judy wrote one day: "They say [the bull's] wild and dangerous. He just looks lost to me."

Now tell me, don't you think that's exactly what Jesus would have posted on Facebook* about this bull? Isn't that how he sees this bull?

And don't you think this is exactly how he sees each of his children? Not wild and dangerous, not scared and alone, not unworthy or ungrateful, but lost. And in need of a little pat on the hide and a pull home.

Of course, like Mike, Judy certainly didn't type these words as instruction for living mercy, but since she is also a walking example of "How to Love People and Live Mercy," my brain filed this under its ever-expanding "mercy" file.

When we seek out the more-to-the-story that lies behind every person and every circumstance, we begin to see things the way Jesus does.

I think this is a reminder that while the world tends to see bulls and situations and people *one* way, Jesus calls us to see differently. And the lens through which we're to view the world is one of mercy and grace. One that enables us to see this world as a place full of lost, scared people, in need of a Savior, certainly, but also one full of ways that we can act as the hands and feet of Jesus and make a difference. A world that we can love and that we can transform. Where we can help the lost get found and the scared get soothed.

Now tell me this: What if we used this mercy filter in all the situations of life where mercilessness tends to flare? What if, every time we got jealous or angry or annoyed, we looked

---

* See, Mom? Facebook = working!

for the "more" to the story? What if we always tried to see things as Jesus would—through the lenses of grace and love and mercy?

What if, every time we got jealous or angry or annoyed, we looked for the "more" to the story?

After trying it—on everyone from crabby wait staff to tired kids—I can tell you that it changes the way you view or relate to everyone around you. It changes the way you think about people, the way you feel. That's true whether you need to show more mercy to a family member or your mean neighbor or the person who annoys you or the person who hurt you deeply.

Showing—and living—mercy changes lives. Yours as well as those around you.

Mercy and Justice

Throughout this whole chapter, a part of me kept throwing an elbow and whispering, "But, what about . . . ?" and "But mercy doesn't mean we have to . . . ." This is the firstborn, rule-loving, justice-oriented part of me. I've hushed and shooed her away until now—but since she has some valid points, I'll let her speak a minute.

Showing mercy doesn't mean we have to let people totally off the hook. It *can*, certainly. Sometimes showing mercy involves leniency in punishment or consequence. A last-minute call from a governor staying an execution is mercy. That said, releasing a guilty, convicted, dangerous murderer from prison and letting him back onto the street would be too much mercy, which roughly translates to: *stupid*. Foolish, perhaps the Bible would call it. At least as administered by our broken selves.

One could argue that God showed "too much" mercy and let those of us who accept this mercy off the hook when he sent Jesus to pay the price for our sin. And I'm humbled and grateful that he did. Of course, God can do this in his infinite wisdom, faithfulness, and knowledge and have it be good and just, make sense and be loving. But we can actually run into trouble living too much mercy.

For instance, my husband will tell you that I show too much mercy to our kids. And I do. I'm a terrible, inconsistent disciplinarian, and I'm a little too merciful when I see sweet faces saying, "I'm sorry." While showing mercy in the short term might look reasonable, even noble, allowing our kids to grow up *sans* consequences is not merciful. It's horrible. For them. And for society in general.

Establishing rules and enacting consequences for when rules are broken or establishing boundaries over which no one should cross is another facet of love—of others and ourselves. It is mercy. Allowing *anyone* to be abused or walked on is not merciful—even to the abuser. So please don't mistake my call to show mercy as a call to endure mistreatment.

Someday, we'll be held accountable to God in heaven. And before that, God doesn't let us off scot-free from the natural consequences of our actions. When the criminal hanging next to Jesus had his "come to Jesus" moment, Jesus showed mercy—"Today you will be with me in paradise" (Luke 23:43, NIV)—but the criminal stayed right up there on that cross. So did Jesus. God's mercy to us sure didn't look like mercy to Jesus. I suppose that mercy can be complicated.

Not unlike forgiveness. In fact, mercy shares a lot in common with forgiveness. Just as forgiving someone doesn't mean we help break her out of prison or allow a hurtful, potentially dangerous person into our homes or lives, so mercy allows us to draw and keep boundaries and permit people to face consequences for their actions.

Instead, living mercy frees us from thinking we need to be the judge and jury on everything. It stops "get a job" from huffing through our brains as a woman with the "Homeless and Hungry" sign walks toward us at the stoplight. Mercy stops our eyes from rolling and our tongues from *tsk-tsk*-ing that mom as her kids run wild around the store. Mercy means we don't grumble back at our crabby neighbor.

Mercy compels us to be kind, to be fair, to give, to help, to befriend, to talk to, to listen, to bring a meal, to serve, to reach out, to hold, to do whatever we're called to do without rolling our eyes in judgment. Mercy lets us see the planks in our own eyes even as we notice the sawdust in others' (see Matthew 7:3).

Mercy compels us to give, to help, to befriend without rolling our eyes in judgment.

Mercy knows life is hard and that everybody's got problems. Mercy knows that most people just need to be cut some slack. Mercy gives breaks. Mercy offers chances and opportunities. Mercy walks around with a smile on her face and a hand ready to help.

Mercy stops us from criticizing and judging and lashing out at people who disagree with us. Mercy listens to those who think differently, feel differently, and (gasp!) vote differently. Mercy smiles at those who annoy us. Mercy looks for the other side of the story. Mercy doesn't see as the world sees, but as Jesus does.

Mercy doesn't yell at her mom on the phone because she makes a noise. Mercy doesn't berate her husband because he's late—again. Mercy doesn't snap at her kids because she's tired and they've got too much energy. Mercy doesn't leave mean notes on the windshields of cars of moms who park in the *fire lane* at her kids' school. (Although I'm pretty sure mercy calls the police department and has *them* leave their own little yellow notes. My kids are in that building, after all!)

And mercy shows herself again and again and again—which is the hardest part of mercy. It's easy to show mercy once. Twice, even. But again and again? To that person who makes you nuts? To that person who just won't get a job? Who won't get help? Who won't go to rehab? Who won't say she's sorry?

Mercy keeps on showing up for all of them too. Because we need to draw boundaries and allow consequences, mercy may only show itself in the way we think about or look at another person or situation. But even that kind of mercy makes all the difference. It may be too dangerous for mercy to drag the bull back to his farm, but seeing him as lost and scared rather than mean and wild changes everything about his rescue.

Because we need to draw boundaries and allow consequences, mercy may only show itself in the way we think about or look at another person or situation.

What's in It for Me?

When it comes to loving your life, I'm not sure anything has a bigger "payoff" than living mercy. This is tacky to talk about, but it's true nonetheless. Not only does living mercy allow you to change the lives of those around you—by meeting needs, by giving chances, by cutting slack—but it changes your life too. Mercy makes you love life. While I never believe that happiness is itself an end goal, mercy makes you happy. Mercy warms hearts and brings joy.

Look at the opposite: Living mercilessly is a horrible way to live. Merciless is a horrible kind of person to be! Merciless people are bitter, crabby, mean, joyless, paranoid, dangerous even. This sounds extreme. But think of yourself when you fail to exhibit mercy. I've certainly become all these things. I see these qualities in the merciless people I encounter. And I encounter them all the time. You need to understand something: Writers engage in one of the few occupations on earth for which other people are actually paid to criticize them. People make livings saying bad things (and good things) about what other people pour their hearts and minds and souls into. And now that blogs exist, people will gladly do this for free. Lovely.

In all seriousness, I'm glad these people exist. Critique helps us all improve. Feedback on what we write or say keeps us thinking and searching. For the most part, I'm a fan of blogs and the ability to comment on articles. I love the dialogue. I love the ideas they generate. I've stolen a lot of ideas for this very book from such comments. So thank you.

There's another part I don't love, though: the meanness. And even on (make that, especially on!) Christian sites, people get mean. Merciless. In responses to things I've written, I've been slammed by all sorts of ugly, awful, stinking, dirty types of discourse.

I've been told I'm a bad mom, a bad wife, a bad Christian. A bad writer, a bad speller (which is true), and a wrong thinker. I've been told I'm selfish and stupid. That I'm bound for hell and that I'll be taking all sorts of my innocent readers with me. And I've been told all this by people who sign their names "in Jesus."

I'm not the only writer (or artist or actor or pastor or thinker) facing this. Ask one you know. Or visit my writers group. Then you'll hear story after story of one of us being accosted and accused by readers or listeners who disagree with us and who think we'll burn in hell for what we've written. It's so nice

While many of us writers have tough skins and can "handle" this, it's still hard. And it still hurts. And it still stinks. I've spent a lot of time angry at my critics, and I've spent a lot of time typing back cutting comments telling them how wrong they are. Because, you know, I have a right to defend myself.

But the thing is, every time I did, after the sweetness of vengeance faded, I felt so gross and ugly. So rotten and bitter. After one particularly delicious comeback of mine, the guilt hit faster than usual. "Vengeance is mine, sayeth the Lord," echoed through my brain.

I couldn't remember if it was biblical or one of those things people say to sound biblical, so I looked it up. Indeed it is biblical. Straight outta Romans 12:19, which says:

Dear friends, never take revenge. Leave that to the righteous anger of God. For the Scriptures say,

> *"I will take revenge;*
> *I will pay them back,"*
> *says the LORD.*[29]

That's mercy. Giving our revenge over to God. But in my biting comments, I had taken it myself. I had been equally mean, equally merciless. When mercy showed up, she reminded me to look for the stories behind those mean comments, to see my critics as Jesus sees them.

I resisted at first, but then I understood. These merciless commentators are lost and scared. They all have more to their stories. They deserve mercy just as much as I do—especially those who warn me that my salvation is in jeopardy because of a view I took on, say, working moms. Clearly, they have no concept of grace. And that breaks God's heart—so it ought to break mine.

So now—very imperfectly and often very begrudgingly—I handle mean comments and cruel criticism differently. I take a lot of deep breaths, I walk away for a while, and I pray—for those offending me and for myself. I ask that any response I make will be done in love and mercy (I have been known to pray that God takes speedy revenge, but I try not to). Then, if I still feel I need to respond (because responding can be a justice issue), I do so with mercy.

While it's not as instantly delicious to type a merciful response—especially when I know I could obliterate someone with words—mercy's sweetness lasts and actually increases with time. Mercy never turns bitter. It's a gift to everyone involved. And it's a great way to live.

OKAY, GOD:

It's so much easier to judge. It's so much easier to be hard on others—especially with my life as hard as it is right now. It's hard to show mercy. But it seems as though you probably know something about that. Help me to be merciful. Help me to share your mercy—to give it away as freely as I receive it.

Anyhow, God, Hallelujah.

Amen.

Getting to Hallelujah

Questions for Reflection and Discussion

1. What are situations in which you have failed to show mercy? What was the result? How did it make you feel?

2. Which people are you least likely to show mercy to? Why do you suppose that is?

3. When have you been shown mercy? What has that meant in your own life?

4. Whom do you know who needs mercy right now? What would it look like for you to show mercy? What might be the effect on the recipient? What might be the effect on you? On those around you?

PART IV

Learn a New Hallelujah

CHAPTER 10

LIVE EXPECTANTLY

Letting Go of Your Presumptions

NOT LONG AGO, I broke one of my cardinal rules: I raised my expectations. Allow me to explain.

Our power went out during a storm so violent that my son said, "That storm musta been caused by sin!" I laughed so hard that I couldn't even bring myself to question his shaky theology. I figured I had to cut the kid some theological slack; we had just watched *Evan Almighty*, so the story of Noah and the flood was fresh on his brain. Plus, funny is funny.

But anyway, this sin-caused storm toppled trees and flipped shingles off our roof. The storm dinged our siding with its hail and fury. The wind and the trees felled by lightning knocked down several nearby power lines, leaving live wires slithering across driveways and snaking across side streets and leaving most of my town without power. When I called the electric company, they said it would be *days* until we got our wonder-working power back on.

Days. Ugh.

We'd been through this before, and it had usually, literally been days. So I scrounged up our camping lanterns, found the flashlights and candles, and charged my phone in the car. Then we headed out to watch a river of water flow down our street and to commiserate with neighbors as we assessed the mess. Then we hunkered down. And went to bed early.

The next morning, the same thing. My brain went into "days without power" mode. I plugged our fridge into our kind neighbor's generator, and I packed up my computer and headed out to a spot with WiFi and outlets so I could still forge ahead in my work. And forge ahead I did! I powered on without power. Not expecting to have electricity for days makes you take full advantage of every opportunity you have to hook up.

When I got back home, I called the power company again. After punching in my home phone so they could "access" my account, I got the news: field crews were in our area and the utility company *expected* us to have power by 7 p.m. That night! That wasn't *day-za*. That was a *day-ya*.

I think I yelled, "WooHoo!"

And therein lies my big mistake: I *believed* the power company. I *expected* them to be right. I *expected* to have power back by 7 p.m. And puh-leese, if I was getting power back on at seven, why was I still sitting there writing? I had all night. I was fine. The more I thought about how much time I had, the more I realized I was hungry. And in the mood to take a walk, to see which trees were *still* down.

So I stopped working. My productivity ceased. My changed expectations changed me. My *heightened* expectations took me and my mood right up with it. I was on top of my powerless world.

And therein lies the other problem: I let heightened expectations heighten my mood. Whenever I (or any of us) do this, when we let our moods rise on what we expect, we set ourselves up for all sorts of trouble. For failure. For crashes.

And that's just what happened. Seven o'clock came and went. No power. And I crashed. I beat myself up over lost time. I was miserable. Seven o'clock the next morning came and went. And I stayed crashed. My mood skidded right on down the steep hill of expectations I had so happily climbed the day before.

When we let our moods rise on what we expect, we set ourselves up for all sorts of trouble. For failure. For crashes.

Now, on the list of crashes that a person can experience because of expectations set too high, regaining power certainly is no "topper." Most of us crash from heightened expectations on *life*, yet the theory behind it is the same. If we expect too much or expect the wrong things, we're doomed for disappointment. We're destined to be dissatisfied with the people or the circumstances of our lives. We're bound to be blue if we set our expectations too high.

I realize even as I type these words that many of you will read this and just feel sad for me and my gloomy outlook. I don't blame you. In fact, I was once just like you. Until I learned what the Danes know.

Great Danes

Years ago researchers conducted a study to find the happiest people on earth. The findings got lots of press and caught the attention of a lot of people. Among them, me.[30] The study's revelation shocked and rocked me.

Honestly, it's changed the way I live. Certainly the way I approach my birthday and days like Mother's Day. It definitely helps when sending off book proposals or pitching articles. Frankly, while again I don't consider "happiness" to be a goal in life, when I do remember to employ this "trick," I gotta tell you, I am happier.

Here's what the study found: The Danish are the happiest people on earth because they go through life with—you guessed it—low expectations! They don't dream big and they don't expect much. This way, anything good that happens is icing on the Danish, if you will. Simple as that.

Now, since the small part of me that is not Swedish is in fact Danish, I glommed on to the wisdom of my people like nobody's business. Even though it could not run more contrary to the way I was raised. Even by my part-Danish mother. I was raised in the red-blooded, hard-working American-dream fashion to expect certain—if not *big*—things.

Still today, I like to agree with Walt Disney and his "if you can dream it, you can do it" optimism. And the Jesus follower in me knows that we ought to have some expectations for ourselves and for others.

But it seems that the Danes discovered the trouble with expectations—or at least high ones—long ago. High expectations disappoint. They leave us confused and often desperate.

The expectations that we put on our lives—and that *others* put on our lives—drive many of us crazy. But it's not only the unmet expectations that do this. It's the lies that surround expectations—the false promises of the "if-thens" that we're told.

And these lies fly at us from all over the place: from our culture, from our families, and from our Christian communities. If we're going to learn to love our lives—as God intended them to be—we have to look at what's been expected of us and what we've expected. Then we must learn to separate the truth from the lies. The good expectations from the bad.

Good Expectations

In the chapter on mercy, I confessed to being a terrible disciplinarian to my kids. It's true. I totally blame my parents for this. They weren't into discipline either. I got spanked maybe twice. Mouth washed out once. Yelled at? Well, probably plenty. Maybe I got the keys to my car taken away? Maybe not.

What I did get was the guilt of *knowing* when I had disappointed them. I got the chilly shoulders of letdown when I knew I hadn't met their expectations for and of me.

I still don't know how they did it. Their method of parenting was to lay out the things they expected from me and then sort of set them out there, dangling, a few steps ahead and above as I navigated my growing up. I'm never sure whether my heeding these expectations meant that I was shame based or guilt based, but whatever I was based in, I never wanted to disappoint them, so I tried hard to meet their expectations:

- That I would work hard in school.
- That I would look presentable. (Beyond presentable, really. You should have seen me. I was ridiculously beautifully outfitted.)
- That I wouldn't drink or do drugs. In high school.
- That I wouldn't have sex. In high school.

- That I wouldn't talk back.
- That I'd be polite.
- That I'd go to college.
- That I'd not get married too young.

I'm sure there were other things. These just come to mind. And really, I pretty much met all these expectations. And they are good ones. Reasonable. In fact, you'll notice some expectations that were *not* on this list. Or some that have qualifiers. That might give you glimpses of where I fell off the wagon later in life.

Don't misunderstand what I'm saying here: parents expecting things of their children is a good thing. God gave us rules—and *expected* us to try and follow them— for good reason. These sorts of expectations keep us safe, keep us sharp, keep us on the road to becoming what God intended us to be. Good, reasonable expectations bring order and sensibility to a broken world. We need expectations.

Even at *The Mommy Revolution*, the site Carla Barnhill and I founded largely to counter all the oppressive expectations we tend to place on mothers, we spell out what we think a good mom should do and be. In our "Revolutionary Manifesto" on the expectations of a mom, we write: "A good mom provides food, shelter, clothing, love, support, encouragement, and all the honesty, wisdom, and kindness she can. Everything else—rides to the mall, attendance at soccer games, participation in endless rounds of Pretty Pretty Princess—is gravy."[31]

While this probably doesn't seem all that "revolutionary,"

to us it was. Because we're pretty anti-expectations at *The Mommy Revolution*. Or, I should say, we're all about changing, broadening, throwing the doors open on expectations.

Mostly because while this whole "this isn't how it's supposed to be!" part of life hits everybody at different times for different reasons, for my friend Carla and me, the expectations about motherhood had everything to do with it.

Bad Expectations

I did not spend my growing-up years playing with dolls or pining for the days I'd walk down the aisle and then cradle my own baby in my arms. And even though I was married more than four years before it ever even dawned on me that we might want to have a child, I fully bought into the expectation that motherhood would "fulfill" me.

After all, I was told that school would fulfill me. And it did. I was told working would fulfill me. And it did. Sure, I was told following Jesus would fulfill me and had realized some issues with that along the way, but I figured it was just me (more on this later). So when I decided to leave my low-paying but fulfilling magazine-editing job to "stay home" with my son, I expected to be just as fulfilled in my days at home as I had been in my days at work.

At first, I was. What's not fulfilling about lounging on the sofa, snuggling a scrumptious newborn, and catching up on reruns? What's not fulfilling about enjoying long strolls, and pointing out trees and squirrels to a clueless but gurgly boy? That's good stuff!

But as the years went on—even as I took on freelance writing and editing work—I realized something horrible: motherhood didn't fulfill me.* I once described being a mom as "boring" to a friend over coffee. From her slack jaw and her scrunched eyebrows, I thought my friend was going to throw her coffee at me and storm off. Instead, she paused a few beats and then said, "Yes! Motherhood *is* boring."

The feeling that I was a horrible human for not being fulfilled by "a woman's highest calling" started me on a mission to chuck what the world and what the church expected of me and to seek out what God expected.

My friend's words affirmed my realization that motherhood didn't fulfill as I'd been led to believe—and as I'd expected. That turned out to be one of the best breakthrough moments of my life.

For a while I wallowed in the feeling that I was a horrible human for not being fulfilled by what some (wrongly) describe as "a woman's highest calling." Still, this season of my life started me on a massive search for the "real me," who felt very lost. (For another two hundred or so pages on this, see my first book, *Mama's Got a Fake I.D.* No really, get it. You'll love it. Really. Good stuff, if I do say so myself.) It also started me on a mission to chuck what the *world* and what the *church* expected of me and to seek out what *God* expected. And wow. Those are all different things.

---

*Remember the chapter on mercy? Remember how I said I get mean e-mails and comments? This is the sort of stuff I get it for. Even if you're flush with anger and hatred toward me, remember: *mercy.*

What They Expect

As Christians, we like to think we are *different* from the rest of the world. But really? Honestly? Most of the time, not so much. Or, I should say, we North American Christians are very different from the rest of the world, but not so different from *our* neck of the world.

Our culture expects that if we go to a good school and work hard, we'll get a good job and be great. And if we marry the "right" person, we'll be set. Culture expects us to procreate and to be productive members of society. Each generation, in fact, is expected to "do better" than the one before. The church nods right along with this. Don't we?

Each generation, in fact, is expected to "do better" than the one before. The church nods right along with this. Don't we?

Apparently our expectations for behavior aren't all that different either. While we may *try* to do better, in reality, we lust after people and stuff, just the same. We waste and we pollute, just the same. We become addicted to drink or drugs or gambling or porn, just the same. We yell at our kids and flip off other drivers, just the same. We fight with our spouses or divorce them altogether, just the same.

While some items on our lists of expectations may differ, we still offer them just the same. And often those presuppositions lack a clear view of God's purpose for an individual person just the same. We like carbon-copy expectations and clear results and rewards just the same.

This happens to men and to women, to moms and to dads, to singles and to marrieds, to those childless by choice and to those wrestling with infertility. To the young and to the old; to the extroverted and to the introverted; to the smart and to the dumb; to the healthy and to the sick. We expect the same. That is, for God to work the same.

Think about it. Think about the stories we tell, the promises we make, the expectations we lay out when we're "sharing the gospel." We tell of addicts finding Jesus and never needing another hit. We tell of the homeless finding Jesus and landing a nice place to live, of the jobless finding Jesus and jobs, of the depressed finding Jesus and joy.

Right? And those are great promises. Those are good selling points. I believe they have happened—and they do happen. All the time. But sometimes they don't happen. Often, they don't happen.

You know when our financial disasters started? Just a year—a year!—after we committed to "driving our stake" lifestyle-wise and giving more than we spent. Within a year after promising God that we knew we'd been blessed beyond our needs and that we'd set an income "need" level and give away everything after that.

Shouldn't that be blessed? Isn't that what we tell people to expect? Isn't that what we hear in every sermon on giving? But to be fair: isn't that what the Bible says? God seems pretty clear in Malachi 3:10, when he says, "'Bring the whole tithe into the storehouse, that there may be food in my house. Test me in this,' says the LORD Almighty, 'and see if I will not throw open the floodgates of heaven and pour out so much blessing that there will not be room enough to store it'" (NIV).

The thing is, we expected our blessing to be financial. Who wouldn't? We'll talk about this later in the book, but

we learned (over the years) that the blessings that poured out
from the floodgates of heaven were not in fact shiny gold
or leafy green paper, but another, better kind. But that's not
what we're told to expect.

We're told that accepting Jesus and following God will give
us good *things*. That we will have the "good life." But we've put
the wrong expectations on the good life. We look at it wrong.

My former colleague Todd Hertz wrote this in a post at
ThinkChristian. I loved it so much I wanted to print it out
and hug it:

> Obviously God does want us to obey the life
> instructions in his Word out of love—he knows the
> way to better, less harmful results in our sin-soaked
> world. He knows handling our finances his way will
> yield more resources with which we can do his work.
> And he knows sexual purity can prevent pain and create
> a certain marital bond. But I fear that our rhetoric can,
> at times, make this the point. Instead, those results
> are a side benefit. Not the reason. Obeying God is the
> reason. Living so our focus is him is the reason. Setting
> ourselves apart from the world to let him shine is the
> reason. Obeying God because it draws us nearer to him
> and helps us care about what he cares about should be
> and is enough—regardless of the outcome.
>
> When we try to prove that God's way "works,"
> we can actually create an obstacle to the message. If
> a guy tithes expecting the storehouses to open and
> put him in the lap of luxury, what happens to his
> perception of God when he instead gets laid off? If a

teen experiments with sex and discovers nothing bad happens—and it actually feels just fine outside of marriage—could his or her perception of God's Word be lessened? Or, on the other hand, if a person remains a virgin and is totally disillusioned by marital sex, he or she may wonder, "This was the reward?"

No, the "reward" is being in union with God. The reward is obedience in and of itself. The reward is being in God's will despite what happens next.[32]

I love the idea that the reward of our following God and obeying him is "being in union with God." It's beautiful, and it's the expectation that we *should* have of a life spent following Jesus. It's the reward for the woman who loves her kids and loves being a mom but finds fulfillment plunking out words on a little laptop. It's the reward for the woman who can't kick her addiction no matter how much she loves Jesus. It's the reward for the man who wallows in depression even as his heart cries out to God to lift him up. It's the reward for the emaciated mom rocking a dying toddler in her arms. It's the reward of a hard-wrought life. It's the best thing to expect and to hope for.

Hope Wins

Since I'm a proud alum of Calvin College, whose archrival is Hope College, typing the words *Hope Wins* wouldn't normally be a joy. But it is. Because it does. Hope wins. Over and over again. Even when it's hard to believe, especially considering all I've just written about dashing our own expectations.

Now allow me to play my own devil's advocate again.

You'll see that it's difficult to be a writer, trying to *persuade* and influence and be *me* at the same time! But it is important that we explore all sides here.

As I start to consider hope—get all hopped up on hope, we might say—that old familiar anti-Danish logic starts rumbling back in my head. The "old me" logic that says we should go through life with expectations. That all I've just written is not right or good, because of course God wants us to have expectations. We expect God to show up. We expect the Holy Spirit to fuel us. We expect Jesus to come back. All rightfully so.

That's a different kind of expecting though, is it not? We can and should expect from God. However, those expectations still require patience and a willingness to expect some mystery from him. That's why I think the Bible tosses out the word *hope* so much. That's what we're called to do. That's what we need to hang on to.

While hope keeps her eyes on the same future that expectation does, hope looks ahead differently. And hope feels different in our lives. Hope presents herself differently— more elegantly.

Hope is a longing. Expectation is a demand. Hope admits frailty and uncertainty and teetering trust. Expectation thumps a fist and exerts power. Hope is a virtue. Expectation—in most circumstances, probably—is a vice.

Hope admits frailty and uncertainty and teetering trust. Expectation thumps a fist and exerts power.

When lived out, expectation gruffs and pants and paces. Hope smiles and stills and waits. Expectation keeps eyes focused on the road ahead. Hope turns her head toward heaven, fixing her "gaze on things that cannot be seen" (2 Corinthians 4:18), and takes in the fuller view.

Expectations let us down, leave us hanging. Hope lifts us up, sends us flying. Expectations disappoint. Hope, the Bible tells us, does not.

How great is this passage from Romans 5 (NIV):

Therefore, since we have been justified through faith, we have peace with God through our Lord Jesus Christ, through whom we have gained access by faith into this grace in which we now stand. And we boast in the hope of the glory of God. Not only so, but we also glory in our sufferings, because we know that suffering produces perseverance; perseverance, character; and character, hope. And hope does not put us to shame, because God's love has been poured out into our hearts through the Holy Spirit, who has been given to us. (vv. 1-5)

What I love about what's packed into these few verses (and there's a lot!) is the journey toward hope. What it takes to get there. It is *in* and *through* our sufferings and disappointments, through the agony or disillusionment from unmet expectations that we become more of who God made us to be. It's how we learn to persevere, how we develop character, and how we begin to lay down our expectations and live with hope.

After we let it all out, lay it all down, hope wins. Let's take a look how to get there.

OKAY, GOD:

Life wasn't supposed to be like this. You know I feel this way from earlier grumblings. But it's confusing: I did so much preparation for life to go a certain way and this just isn't what I expected. Please take those expectations. Give me new ones. Ones that match your will for my life. Fill me with the hope that comes from knowing that you delight in every detail of my life—and from walking along this unexpected path with you.

Anyhow, God, Hallelujah.

Amen.

Getting to Hallelujah
Questions for Reflection and Discussion

1. What does your family—your parents, spouse, kids, siblings—expect of you? As you were growing up, what did you expect from yourself? your life?

2. What does your church and community expect from you?

3. What influence do these expectations have on your life?

4. What are some of your unmet expectations?

5. What are some of the things you hope for?

CHAPTER 11

LIVE DEAD

Letting Go of Your Own Life

THE HEADLINE drew me in: "John Edwards' Daughter: Our Lives Were 'Savaged.'" But I zeroed in on one word: *savaged*. While the reasons why my life has felt *savaged* differ from those of the disgraced senator's family, the word works well. Whenever I've looked around at what seems like a tattered, faded remnant of the happy, vibrant life I once enjoyed, it indeed appears *savaged*.

Cate Edwards, the daughter who shared this in an essay for *People* magazine, wrote about her mother: "There are things she taught without words. . . . [Like] how to continue to live your life on your own terms when it somehow becomes savaged by people you never invited into it."[33]

The idea of a life being savaged by someone else is downright depressing. No doubt about this. I've been there. You, too, probably. And it's hard to figure out how to live on your "own terms" or (better yet) on God's terms after this has happened. A life savaged by another *person* is tough to recover from.

But what if you get the niggling sense—as I've had—that it's not so much about another *person* who's savaged your life as much as maybe *God.* Yikes. This isn't fun to admit. Out loud. In public. It sounds too harsh. Or loony. Or heretical. God is supposed to be our Savior, not our Ruiner.

And yet, last summer as I stood frozen with fear at the end of a high dive, I realized what God probably already knows: that sometimes getting people to do something often takes a bit of a push—or a threat.

It all started with me wanting to show my kids that they had nothing to be afraid of with the high dive at our local pool. As long as you could swim to the sides, I told them, you'll be safe as can be.

So I decided to *model* fearlessness for them. Though it had been twenty years since I last jumped off a high dive, during adult swim I situated my kids on pool chairs by the lifeguard stand at the dive pool and marched over to the high dive. I climbed the ladder, rung by rung, like a trouper. Like a big brave girl, I stepped out onto the platform, each step a little bouncier than the last. Then I made my mistake. I—say it with me—looked down. And I froze.

Oh, God, I prayed quickly as my kids waved with big smiles from below, *I can't do this. I can't jump. Help.*

I turned back, hoping no one was behind me in line, so I could just graciously escape. I could fake a lost contact or something. My kids would understand.

But alas, a man was already almost all the way up the ladder, holding firm on the arm rails as he waited.

I tried to will myself off. I tried to bounce again and just look forward. Again, I prayed, *God, get me out of this. I can't jump.*

Then I heard, from behind, in a thick Eastern European accent, "Don't be afraid. Just step off."

I turned to him. "I don't think I can."

"You can," he said. "Don't be afraid. Just go."

"I can't."

"If you're too scared, I can push you."

As I type the story now I realize this sort of threat deserved—at the very least—a stern whistle from the lifeguard, but at the time, it was just what I needed to hear. I didn't want this guy pushing me in, and it didn't look like he was going to budge off that ladder. So I waved one more time to my kids, looked straight ahead, and jumped.

And it was horrible. The water smacked my side hard! My eyes burned with the chlorine that forced its way in. And my bathing suit bottom rode further up than I thought possible and the top, well, it had to be adjusted quickly.

But I did it. My kids were so proud—even if none of them wanted to try it themselves.

When the Eastern European pusher-man pulled himself up out of the water, he smiled and congratulated me. Then he said, "Next time maybe you won't need to be pushed."

I didn't bother telling him there would be no next time.

Now, I hate to go overspiritualizing every last thing. I'm still not sure how me jumping off a high dive added anything of real value to my life. But what I do know is that when I prayed up there, asking God for help—for rescue, really—along came someone who wasn't going to let me chicken out. Who pressed me to step off from all that was comfortable and jump into that which might sting a bit—and leave me decidedly uncomfortable. God's answer to my prayer wasn't that I stay cozy, but that I risk it.

As it happened, not long before my life started unraveling, before my life was savaged, I had prayed. In one of those drastic, crazy prayers, I told God that I was tired of my vanilla life, that I wanted to *follow* him, that I wanted to go where he sent me, that I wanted to be fearless and mighty, that I wanted to live as the woman he made *me* to be and not the person culture or my family or anyone else thought I should be.

God's answer to my prayer wasn't that I stay cozy, but that I risk it.

Looking back, I can see without a doubt that God took me up on that prayer (again, watch what you pray for, people!). But he had to do some work first. Some stuff had to go. He had to get me out on the end of a diving board and maybe give me a bit of a shove.

While I know he didn't cause my parents to split up or strike my dog dead as punishment or clap his hands for other icky things to happen along the way, I think he may have something to do with some of the "bad" stuff. Like, say, our finances.

Because when I prayed that prayer, when I knelt on the ground and asked that God take me and use me, he needed to take a lot of stuff *away* from me. A lot of things about me had to die—violently—before I could be reborn or rebuilt as the person God made me to be. To do the things he would ask of me. And there was no way I would have willingly killed off those things myself. No way I would have ever chosen comparative poverty. No way I would have chucked all my different forms of security out the window on my own. I was not willing to live dead to these things, as we're essentially asked to do.

Matthew 10:39 says, "If you cling to your life, you will lose it; but if you give up your life for me, you will find it." I was clinging while asking God to help me find life in him. It's not supposed to work that way.

While I wasn't really willing to give it up, God loved me enough to come on in and take it. Savage it, if you will. This sounds violent—and awful—to be describing God this way. But it's not that "out there." Take a peek at Job. Or Naomi. Or Jacob. Or his brother, Esau. Or Jesus. God has been known to "take away" even from those he loves like crazy to get his job done.

A lot of things about me had to die—violently—before I could be reborn or rebuilt as the person God made me to be.

Knock, Breathe, Shine

My favorite sonneteer, John Donne, writes about God savaging us—and our resistance—in his famous fourteenth sonnet. I hope you've read it—at least in high school—but it's too good not to allow you to read again.

> *Batter my heart, three-personed God; for you*
> *As yet but knock, breathe, shine, and seek to mend;*
> *That I may rise and stand, o'erthrow me, and bend*
> *Your force to break, blow, burn, and make me new.*
> *I, like an usurped town, to another due,*
> *Labor to admit you, but O, to no end;*
> *Reason, your viceroy in me, me should defend,*
> *But is captived, and proves weak or untrue.*
> *Yet dearly I love you, and would be loved fain,*
> *But am betrothed unto your enemy.*

Divorce me, untie or break that knot again;
Take me to you, imprison me, for I,
Except you enthrall me, never shall be free,
Nor ever chaste, except you ravish me.[34]

While I've read this a million times, until I was battered a bit by our three-personed God, I never fully appreciated this poem. Even as I studied this in English 201-ish during college, when I certainly lived much of my life as if I were "betrothed unto your enemy," the citations in my anthology don't reflect any kind of connection to the poem other than appreciating its meter, its form, and its language.

I scrawled out *violent imagery* in the margin next to the opening lines. I printed *a, b, b, a, a, b, b, a, c, d, c, d, c, d* to mark the rhyme pattern. I noted that it was the devil John wanted to divorce from and that "break that knot *again*" indicates a continuous problem. But then at the end, I wrote, "*rape?*" I do remember being shocked and appalled that John Donne would compare what God can do to a life with something as heinous as being ravished—or raped.

I still do, actually. And I'm not sure that had a woman written this sonnet she would have chosen the same word. I certainly wouldn't. Rape is pure evil. God is pure good.

But still. Now that my own life has been savaged, my own heart battered, I get what John Donne means. And I get why he'd tell God to take him—forcefully. To imprison him. To break his heart. To overthrow him. To break the ties that bind him to Satan.

Because that life—the one where we love God (as John Donne did, as I do, as I hope you do) but still find ourselves trotting after what Satan offers—stinks. It doesn't bless—in the ways that really matter. It leaves us empty, lonely, sad. It leaves us hating life.

Which brings me back to Matthew 10:39 and its "counterpart" in John. If any passage has troubled me during the writing of a book on "how to love your life," it's John 12:25: "Those who love their life in this world will lose it. Those who care nothing for their life in this world will keep it for eternity."

This certainly makes it seem like having a goal of "loving life" would run counter to Scripture. At least at face value. But the same Jesus who said this also said we should love others as we love *ourselves.* I'm pretty sure that Jesus expects us to love ourselves—a lot. The verse doesn't mean that we only have to love others a little bit because we're not supposed to love ourselves—or our lives—in this world.

We need to be willing to let go of our own understanding of what's supposed to be *and grab hold of what God has in store.*

I've come to realize that John 12:25 means that we can't love our lives in ways that make us grip and cling to the lives *we* imagined or as our world, our families, or our churches led us to *expect* them to be. We need to be willing to let go of our own understanding of what's *supposed to be* and grab hold of what God has in store.

We need to die to this life. We need to live dead. Cheery, huh?

But look at how *The Message* translates John 12:25:

Listen carefully: Unless a grain of wheat is buried in the ground, dead to the world, it is never any more than a grain of wheat. But if it is buried, it sprouts and reproduces itself many times over. In the same way, anyone who holds on to life just as it is destroys that life. But if you let it go, reckless in your love, you'll have it forever, real and eternal.

This offers us the truth and the blessing and the *hope* of living dead. Of laying down and burying our expectations, our worldly desires, our lusts and longings, our fears and failures, our triumphs, our successes, our wealth, our dreams, our ideas, our everything. When they die as they are—as *we* have created them—and we bury them, burn them, and offer them to God, we get to see God doing his thing. We get to see resurrections. We get to see new life—in him. We get to see God raise up our expectations, our worldly desires, our lusts and longings, our fears and failures, our triumphs, our successes, our wealth, our dreams, our ideas, our everything. We get to see God in all of them. As he defines them. As he would have them.

> *We get to see God raise up our expectations, our worldly desires, our lusts and longings, our fears and failures, our triumphs, our successes, our wealth, our dreams, our ideas, our everything.*

This is *kenosis*. What you will give up— empty of yourself—for Jesus. For God. Giving up, going down, so you can be raised again. My friend Gregg said in a sermon once, "God isn't done performing resurrections." Of course he's not. We see it happen all the time. Goodness, look at nature. If you live in a cold-winter climate, you understand this well—and see it occur every year. It's why spring is pure magic, why those first blooms and buds, why the greening of the grass, why those first sweet smells restore us like nothing else. But we also understand that this is why fall and winter need to happen. To be resurrected, to be reborn, something has to die. It's the same in our own lives.

Because we aren't Jesus, our being resurrected doesn't mean that life goes on perfectly. But life goes on better when we let go—when we release our grips on the things we think matter—and, as they say, let God.

What to Release

I'm not huge into fishing. I'm not into it at all, actually—though I like the part where you get to sit by water. I'll do anything that means my butt or my feet are planted within a foot or two of a lake or a pond or a stream.

However, my kids and my husband like it. So I'm involved in it enough to know how to hook a worm and how to gut and fry a catfish, among other things. As I type, leeches (leeches!) swim in a tiny Styrofoam bowl in my fridge (*in* my fridge!).

That said, the worst part of fishing is not the worms or the gutting or even the leeches. It's pulling out a hook and tossing back a fish that's too small or unacceptable for whatever reason. To be honest, I find it more cruel than even yucky.

Which is not to say I don't *get* why fisherfolk need to do this. While I do think it's cruel when people fishing "for fun"* yank and toss back every fish they catch into the water, I do understand why some fish need to go back. As horrible as it is to know that some fish swim the waters with hooks still snagged into their lips or stuck in their guts, and as much as

---

*That is, without intending to eat them. Yes, this means I also think it's cruel to fish for sport and then mount your catch. This takes our dominion over animals a bit far. So wasteful and scornful of God's creation.

I hate to think of the pain they suffer when a barbed hook is ripped from their flesh, I understand. Some fish have to be tossed back because they're too young. Or they're threatened or endangered. They need to be cast back for the species to prosper, to be fruitful and multiply. If no one throws the fish back, the species will die off—and the purpose of their existence along with it. The fish must be thrown back, hooks, scrapes, blood, and all, so they can live and prosper.

It's sort of the same with us. Just like those fisherfolk, we need to know what we should throw back—throw down at the feet of Jesus, at the foot of the Cross, at the base of the throne (use whichever image works for you). The point is, we need to identify those areas of our lives that need to be given up, thrown back. The things we need to be emptied of. We need to look at the things of life we love and cling to, and let them go.

Of course, just a couple of pages back, I said we need to lay down *everything*. And we do. Eventually. But if we just pray, "God, I lay down everything" it feels, well, as weak and pointless as if we prayed, "God, I ask you for everything!"

The power and beauty of kenosis is found in the specificity and intentionality of the act of what we're tossing back to God, of what we're willing to sacrifice. Because then we can see what God chooses to give back, to resurrect. And we can cling to God and his gifts.

When I surveyed my life and looked for things I needed to empty myself of, the first thing I knew had to go was my materialism. In the "Live Gladly" chapter, we talked about driving your stake and declaring when enough is enough. That's what emptying yourself of materialism looks like. It's saying, "The way I view *stuff* stinks. You give me a better way." If it's important to God that you care about *stuff*, or at least some stuff, he'll resurrect it in you. His way.

But for me, I have to tell you, much of my longing for things has stayed good and dead. Sure, some of my formerly materialistic self pops up every now and then, but the constant longing and striving still lies packed solid in the ground.

I'm so grateful. One of the specific areas of materialism I tossed back at God was my house lust. I love houses. I'm the sort who sees a picture-perfect home, eyes its wraparound porch, its white clapboard siding, its shutters, and thinks, *The people who live there must be so happy.* But beyond that silly fantasy, I just love all different types of homes—old, new, open-floor plans, tight mazes of rooms. I'd love to live in a home with a secret passageway and a back (and front) staircase.

I could go nuts spending my life trying to earn enough to get that. Or I could give up that desire to God. Which I did—actually, which I still do, every time I pass a "dream home." I do it via a simple prayer (which I'll tell you about in a second). I'd still love to have that kind of home, but I've driven my stake—so this means that unless God calls us somewhere else (cheaper) where I could buy that sort of home, I've got to hope God is building me a house in heaven with a secret back staircase. And a lake. (A lake would be great, God. You know the one.)

But my house lust has another problem aside from "simple" materialism. It's rooted in pride (because it would be nice to have others as jealous of my house as I am of other people's!), and it's rooted in a desire to meet our culture's ideal of "doing better than your parents." I've yet to do that—house-wise. And it feels like failure. So I've got to lay that desire down. Over and over again.

Praying It Over

Sort of like the Open-Hand Prayer from back in the jealousy chapter, I actually have a motion prayer that I do when I want to lay down a desire or an expectation or a hope or a fear. I cross my arms and lay each hand on the opposite shoulder. Next I think of the thing or the desire or the relationship I need to hand over, and I say, "God, I've been clinging to _____. Please take it and do with it what you will." And then I let go of my shoulders and extend my arms, uncrossing them as they move forward, with palms upward.

I don't do this to add a little "hocus-pocus" to my prayer life, but to mark it, to be as intentional and deliberate as I can. When I remember, I also write my prayer down, so I remember. And I can see what God has done.

I've prayed this prayer for a zillion areas of my life— my goal is to lay down everything. I've prayed:

God, I've been clinging to my *kids* . . .
God, I've been clinging to my *fears* . . .
God, I've been clinging to my *writing career* . . .
God, I've been clinging to my *husband's [former or potential] career* . . .
God, I've been clinging to my *anger* . . .
God, I've been clinging to our *money* . . .
God, I've been clinging to our *debt* . . .
God, I've been clinging to this *house* . . .
God, I've been clinging to that *school* . . .

God, I've been clinging to *feminism* . . .
God, I've been clinging to *libertarianism* . . .
God, I've been clinging to my *longing for rootedness* . . .

Now some of these prayers—you can probably guess
which ones—are downright terrifying to pray. I've released my
kids to God! Not in the same way Hannah did with Samuel,
but still.

In an interview with *Today's Christian Woman*, singer-
songwriter Sara Groves talked about her son Kirby this way:
"I feared something would happen to him. I'd always told the
Lord, 'Your will, not mine. Take me, make me, break me.' But
when Kirby was born, it seemed impossible to say 'Take him,
make him, break him.' I didn't trust God at that level."[35]

Her sentiments are exactly what make emptying ourselves
to God so terrifying. We need to trust God at a whole new
level.

With regard to my kids, of course, emptying myself of them and offering them to God
didn't mean I stopped loving them or caring for them. I didn't kick them out or stop
packing their lunches. I didn't blow off their
questions or requests with, "Go ask your
heavenly Father!"

What makes emptying ourselves to God so terrifying is that we need to trust God at a whole new level.

I still snuggle them and take them to the
pool. I still stir their chocolate milk and help
them turn their beds into slides. I'm still their mom and take
that role seriously. In releasing them to God, none of the outside stuff changed—but all of the inside stuff did.

What I really tossed back was my crazy sense of control,

my worry about them, my belief that no one in heaven or on earth loved them more or could do better for them than I. And I keep praying this. I keep laying my mothering down, believing that God will resurrect a panic or a stress about them when it's needed. He does. I still run when I hear crying. I still ache when one of my children hurts.

In fact, God has raised my concerns in some areas (like when I discovered my three-year-old has a few cavities), but has all but obliterated them in others. Releasing my kids to God allows me to be a better mom to them because it frees me from things I don't need in my heart and on my mind and frees up room for what *should* be there.

The same thing has happened with the expectations and dreams and desires I've tossed back to God. Whether those are dreams and expectations I've had for myself, for my husband, for my marriage, for my parents, or for anything or anyone else, when I toss them back to God, it frees up tons of space inside. Getting rid of the foolish and worldly notions of what life or people *should* be like—the things that *others* told us to expect or demand or want—leaves so much room for the things that *God* wants there. It allows us to see life or people as God thinks they should be. And that usually looks different.

Desires

I thought I was so cool—like I had discovered something so deep and fresh and new. And then a bunch of people started talking about it. One friend even said "Duh" when I shared my insight with her. But I still don't hear enough people talking about it—and I still think it's cool—so I'm sharing it now.

Psalm 37:4 says this: "Take delight in the LORD, and he

will give you your heart's desires." Most of us grew up reading that as if we love God, he'll give us what we want. Right? And maybe that's the way it's supposed to be read. However, one day, I was reading the whole psalm. It's long—forty or so verses—and lovely. Really. It's like an acrostic poem on how to love the life you're living.

Pretty much smack-dab in the middle of the psalm, it says this: "The LORD directs the steps of the godly. He delights in every detail of their lives. Though they stumble, they will never fall, for the LORD holds them by the hand" (vv. 23-24).

I got caught up in the image of me tripping as I walked along—stumbling like my kids do when we take the dog for walks—and God tightening his grip, maybe giving me a little yank and lift so I can straighten up faster or hit the cement softer. And I just got lost for a while in the love God has for me.

Then I started reading the verse backward. We worship a God who delights in every detail of our lives. Every detail! He directs the steps of the godly! And then I wondered—does he direct our steps and give us our hearts' desires? It seemed weird. So I went all the way back to the "desire" verse and began to wonder: if we delight in the Lord, does he give us whatever we want (a.k.a. our "hearts' desires"), or does he place the desires into our hearts? That's a big difference. If God puts our desires in our hearts, that's a great, life-changing notion.

I e-mailed some pastor/Hebrew-speaking friends about this and got rigmarole on the translation (read: they didn't help). So I may be off—but because of those earlier conversations, I know I'm not alone.

We worship a God who delights in every detail of our lives. Every detail!

What I also know is that when I read this passage today, I hear God saying that if I delight in him—if I lay my desires down, if I die to him, if I empty my desires and expectations to him—he'll give me my desires. He'll resurrect them.

And he has. And he does. And he's so good. If we can trust God enough, we can start loving the life he has for us. We just have to be willing to live it dead. Because when we live it dead, when we toss everything back to God and allow him to resurrect what he wants in our lives, we get to live in the freedom and pleasure of knowing that what we long for has been placed there by God. For me, this means I believe God gave me the desire to write, to read, to hang with my family, to have alone time to think and dream, to have time with friends to talk and dream, to have a marriage built on shared goals. God gave me these desires to be cherished and lived. Mightily and fearlessly.

Torched

In her terrific book, *Angry Conversations with God*, Susan Isaacs writes, "God put me on a barbecue spit and burned off every bit of diseased flesh until there was nothing left but dry bones. Now he is putting new flesh and new breath back into me. . . . God torched my life, and it's the best thing that ever happened to me."[36]

God shoving me off the high dive has been the best thing to happen to me, too. A huge answer to prayer. Which is not to say I want him to keep shoving. I'd love a reprieve. But I also know that without my life being savaged by God, I wouldn't have learned the joy of dying to him. I wouldn't know the benefit of kenosis. I wouldn't be living a life I now (mostly) love. I wouldn't be living anywhere close to what God intended.

If my husband and I hadn't known debt and dire finances, if we hadn't experienced "lag times" in his career, I'd have been too lazy to try to write a book. (It's hard work, requiring patience and persistence. Two things I don't have.) Our situation spurred me

Without my life being savaged by God, I wouldn't have learned the joy of dying to him.

to do what I believe God called me to do. I see that now. If my marriage hadn't gone through such stressful seasons, if my parents hadn't divorced, if I hadn't known what it is to suffer financially, I'd still be locked and loaded in judgmentalism, lacking compassion, understanding, and mercy. I'd still be hard and kind of horrible. I don't want to be that.

Even as I continue to go through rough, rough situations (ones I wish I could share more easily but some of which are not mine alone to share), I find myself clinging, and I know I need to lay it down. I have a hard time seeing—in the midst of the messes—what God may have in store or how he'll be able to work, but since I've known him to be faithful before, I have to trust he'll be faithful again. I'll give God this: He does seem to know what he's doing. Whether we see it or not.

Here's what I keep telling myself and what I'll say to you: Whatever it is that you're clinging to now, lay it down. Empty yourself. Live dead. Then see what God resurrects. And love that life.

OKAY, GOD:

In so many ways, life as I know it has been scorched. Burnt to a crisp. It seems unrecognizable to me. Mostly, I hate this. But I know I'd like it all a lot better if I could see this not as wasteland, but as fertile ground. So please help me see this situation, my scorched life, as you do. Help me see what you're doing in all this. Help me to see the shoots of new life that spring up among the ashes. Help me to see the fresh blooms. Help me to focus not on what's been taken away but on what you're bringing back to life—and what you want to shine on in me.

Anyhow, God, Hallelujah.

Amen.

Getting to Hallelujah
Questions for Reflection and Discussion

1. What has "dying to Christ" meant to you in the past? Do you see it as meaning anything different—or more specific—now? If so, explain.

2. In what ways have you seen your life "savaged"? Have you sensed God behind any of it? How do you respond to that?

3. How would you finish this sentence: "Lord, I've been clinging to _____"?

4. What keeps you from releasing to God some things you ought to release?

5. Have you experienced kenosis in your life? Have you known God to resurrect something in you that you thought was dead?

CHAPTER 12

LIVE ON THE PROMISE

Letting Go of Doubt

I SWEAR, no more than two lines into my son Henrik's year-end, first-grade program, my eyes welled right up. Now, while I may not be a big crier by nature, this is par for the course with me at my kids' church and school programs. It's just that when they're up on that stage looking so cute, singing so sweetly (or not so sweetly, as the case often is when goofiness prevails), the rush of mommy love soaks me in crazy, sappy emotion, and the tears just pour out.

This time, though, the tears weren't about the sap; they were about the song.

Since the title of program was "Standing on the Promises," I should have been prepared. Wow. There's just something about a bunch of first graders—so full of future and hope and promise—singing the old classic hymn "Standing on the Promises" that grabs the heart. It sure grabbed mine.

It wasn't just *their* singing about trusting God and

believing his words that got me, though. It was as if their
voices rose and mingled with the generations of believers who
have shared this trust and sung these stanzas for more than
a century. We're talking about generations who have seen
all kinds of evil, war, poverty, inequality, hunger, death, and
disease; who have lived through more not-supposed-to-be's
in life than we can imagine.

I thought of the people—like my grandmother—who lived
through so much pain and devastation and loss and yet who
kept singing stanzas like

> *Standing on the promises that cannot fail,*
> *When the howling storms of doubt and fear assail,*
> *By the living Word of God I shall prevail,*
> *Standing on the promises of God.*[37]

And now my seven-year-old and his classmates joined this
generational choir—at least in my mind. Their singing this
lyrical profession of deep faith blew me away, did me in. Big
time. As the piano plunked away and little voices fluctuated
between smooth melody and shouty staccato, I prayed that
my son would continue to stand on these promises and to
show this kind of faith. Like his great-grandmother, like his
grandmother, and like . . .

I wanted to add me to that list, but before I could get
there, God's whisper blew behind my prayer: *But why are
my promises so hard for* you *to believe?*

Gulp. *Uhhhh . . .*

Man, how I wish that for once I had a good answer for God!
But like all the other times when he's breezily convicted with

his love and mercy and that sweet, sad smile I imagine him wearing in these moments, all I could think, all I could offer, was my heart, and it said: *I don't know. Why do you make it so hard?* Of course, I realize now that my question *was* my answer.

This moment with God trailed me for weeks afterward. I couldn't shake it. I can talk a big game about things like "hope" and "trust" (I had this chapter planned before I went to my son's program), and I can sing "Standing on the Promises" while standing on my head. But if I'm honest with you and God (and it's pretty useless not to be), I have to admit that I think God does make it hard to believe his promises.

> *I can sing "Standing on the Promises" while standing on my head. But I have to admit that I think God makes it hard to believe his promises.*

Well, wait. Let me back that up: I think God makes it hard to believe *many* of his promises. Not all. In fact, right now I can go through some of the "big promises," and I can find plenty that I can believe without a problem. Take some of the promises sung about that night at my son's program:*

1. "The Promise of a Savior." Do I believe this? Absolutely! God made this promise way back when—to Adam and Eve, of course. And continued promising until he sent his Son, who died and rose again! While this may not be *easy* to believe (and plenty of people think it's *crazy* to believe), I do. Once you experience it, that grace is irresistible, after all.

---

* Thank you to the wonderful first grade teachers at Timothy Christian School for making this so easy for me! Thank you Mrs. Weglarz, Mrs. Schommer, and Mrs. Vander Plas!

2. "The Promise to Never Destroy the World Again."
   No problem believing this one! And I have ever
   since fourth grade, when Salt Creek overflowed
   after massive rains and sewer failure. It flooded my
   town enough that we could canoe in the street (it
   was really fun!). While some of my neighbors lost
   everything (my friend Kelly can tell you how *not*
   fun that was), I saw God keep his promise not to
   destroy the whole world. Since then, we've all seen
   cities and islands obliterated—the devastation almost
   too much to bear—but still I believe. A flood may
   destroy my basement every now and again, but the
   world? No way.

3. "The Promise of a Great Nation." Uh-huh. Yup.
   Those Israelites were great, indeed. (And the people of
   Israel still are.)

4. "The Promise of an Everlasting Kingdom." This
   Kingdom seems far-fetched and sometimes downright
   wacky, but I believe this with everything I've got. I'm
   counting on this to see Jesus, to have restored and
   perfected relationships, and to have everything as it
   is supposed to be—at long last! Call me crazy (or a
   heretic), but I believe this so much that whenever I
   pass a house I take a particular liking to (it usually
   involves white-sided turrets, nooks, crannies, big
   porches, and plenty of lakefront footage), I mention
   it to God. I figure he might need some ideas for what
   my house in his everlasting Kingdom should look like.

5. "The Promise to Be with You." Yeah, he's with me. I know it. (Though it wouldn't hurt if he were a little more obvious every now and again.)

And here's where things started getting dicey for me. Because while I also believe the last two promises listed on the program ("The Promise of Courage" and "The Promise of Wisdom"), as I read about them I felt less, let's just say, *stalwart* about them. Hmmm. Turns out these are exactly the types of promises God was asking me about.

So I started noodling some of God's other promises. Actually, I started Googling some promises too—hoping there'd be an official "God's promises" list. Like the seven deadly sins. Not so. God makes a *lot* of promises in his Word. Instead, after much prayer and some prompting from the Holy Spirit and a few wise friends, I went to three promises that I have underlined in all my Bibles, ones I've read and reread through my longish and crazy life as a Christian. I decided to read each verse, write down my initial (very honest) thought, and then rate it on believability (that is, my ability to believe, not God's ability to deliver)—1 being the lowest, 10 the highest.*

- Proverbs 16:3 (NIV, my eighth-grade class verse**): "Commit to the LORD whatever you do, and your plans will succeed."

  - *My thought: Sometimes.*
  - *Believability rank: 6*

---

*I encourage you to do the same exercise with your favorite promises of God.
**I went to a Christian school. I feel oldish, but am in fact not quite old enough to have gone to school at a time when public schools might have had a class verse!

- Jeremiah 29:11 (NIV): "'For I know the plans I have for you,' declares the LORD, 'plans to prosper you and not to harm you, plans to give you hope and a future.'"

  - *My thought: Prosper me? Like with cash? Ummmm. . . .*
  - *Believability rank: 5*

- Matthew 7:7-11 (NIV): "Ask and it will be given to you; seek and you will find; knock and the door will be opened to you. For everyone who asks receives; the one who seeks finds; and to the one who knocks, the door will be opened. Which of you, if your son asks for bread, will give him a stone? Or if he asks for a fish, will give him a snake? If you, then, though you are evil, know how to give good gifts to your children, how much more will your Father in heaven give good gifts to those who ask him!"

  - *My thought: Whatever. Sure seems like we've got a lot of snakes around here. And I was asking for a fish!*
  - *Believability rank: 3*

Here was my deal: It was easy to believe we could commit our plans to the Lord and "succeed" in eighth grade when we were talking about getting into honors English class. But now, after so much failure, after so many plans committed to God that have flopped—I'm supposed to buy this? And I can believe that God plans to give me hope and a future, but the "prosper" and "not to harm" part? Coulda fooled me!

But I have to admit, my reaction to the ask, seek, and

knock one was a bit more severe. In fact, this verse, these beautiful, touching, powerful words of Jesus, actually made me angry—with him. Because in the context of years of asking, seeking, and knocking, this seems like a bald-faced lie. At the very least, Jesus might have mentioned that we could stand on God's doorstep for years banging away, and then when we get tired, spend several more years just sitting on his stoop, head in hands.*

Jesus, what were you talking about?!?!?!

So that's not exactly a great reaction to this promise from my Jesus—the one I'm so crazy about, so desperately needy for, and, most importantly, from the one who's so crazy about me!

But this was a turning point for me. I needed to realize (and confess) that I don't believe many of God's promises. Specifically, the ones I have to *wait* for. You know what I mean here? It's easy to believe the promises of God—i.e., to trust in him fully—when we're either talking about things we've seen him do enough times in the past that it jacks up the odds of him doing it again. Or, when we have a lot of "control" over the situation. Or when we're pretty sure he's going to act quickly because we can pretty much see his work already happening right up there on the horizon.

> *Jesus might have mentioned that we could stand on God's doorstep for years banging away, and then when we get tired, spend several more years just sitting on his stoop, head in hands.*

---

*Though in *A Grief Observed*, C. S. Lewis says it better than I: "Go to him when your need is desperate, when all other help is vain and what do you find? A door slammed in your face and a sound of bolting and double bolting on the inside. After that silence."

Of course, this presents some huge problems—not the least of which is that trusting only what's probable or what you can see right in front of you isn't really trusting. Not in any way, shape, or form, actually.

Hebrews 11:1-2 (NIV) says, "Faith is confidence in what we hope for and assurance about what we do not see. This is what the ancients were commended for."

Uh, yeah. That's not exactly what I have going on here. You may be in the same boat. Well, what do we do? How do we gain this sort of faith the ancients were commended for? How do we learn to trust and believe the promises of God (and your hard-to-believe ones could be different from mine!) that we struggle with so much?

Learning to Stand

For me, learning to stand, learning to trust, or learning to have faith is all about one thing: learning to wait. And I'm no good at that. (Honestly, I even stopped praying for patience long ago because I know the answer—he just gives you more stuff to wait for!) Most of us aren't good at waiting. When we ask, seek, and knock, we'd like a door opened right away and a big, fat fish presented on a gleaming platter (already scaled and filleted and cooked—or raw, if you prefer a little sashimi) from a smiling God. When we're told we'll be prospered and kept from harm, we'd like it now. When we're told we'll have success, it better come ASAP.

But God is our Almighty Father—not our Almighty Butler. And his visions for our success and his definitions of prosperity and his idea of what giving us fish (not snakes) even *is* are not our ideas. They are better. Where we see prosperity as more zeroes in the account at Charles Schwab,* a newer car, or a bigger house, he may have a little something else in mind. Same goes for his timetable.

Step one of our trusting our infinite, wise, gracious, loving God is believing he will deliver on his promises in his time—the right time. Of course, you've heard this a zillion times—and each time it was as annoying to hear as it is right now. Because waiting is no fun. It's boring, you feel lost, and you get anxious.

That is, if you look at waiting as something *passive.* Which is the way I've always seen it. You know, "There's nothing we can do but wait!" Ugh. It makes me jittery just typing that. But in the time since my son's program, since I've come face-to-face with my lack of faith and hope, I've sought the counsel of godly and been-there-felt-that friends.

Waiting is no fun. It's boring, you feel lost, and you get anxious—if you look at it as something passive.

When I asked them about what standing on the promises of God, what living faithfully and hopefully meant to them, I got a couple of amazing responses. They showed me that waiting doesn't have to be passive or make you feel stuck and icky at all (like we talked about in chapter 4). In fact, hoping and expecting God to turn up in amazing ways is a great way to live life—and a key to loving it. You just have to choose to do it.

Faith and hope and trust and standing on promises are choices we need to make—ones we may have to make every

---

*Just gotta say, I actually believe we are all prosperous money-wise on nearly every global and historical scale!

single day (sometimes every single moment!) but ones so worth making.

My friend Judy Douglass sent me a one-page devotional on this "hopeful choice" issue.* She had written about Psalm 27:13-14 (NIV), which says, "I remain confident of this: I will see the goodness of the LORD in the land of the living. Wait for the LORD; be strong and take heart and wait for the LORD."

Now, most of us don't think of "remain" as a particularly active verb—it sounds kind of *meh*—but considering David had plenty of reasons at this point to kick his confidence to the curb (people trying to kill him, etc.), simply choosing to remain was mighty enough. Yet he goes on and makes some big, hopeful choices.

After going through some of the fuller meanings of the original Hebrew, Judy translates the passage this way:

> There is trouble all around me. Enemies desire to destroy me. But I seek the Lord. And He meets me and rescues me.
>
> Therefore I am confident that my belief/trust in God is firm. I am connected to Him. I can believe that I will see God's goodness in the land of the living as well as in heaven.
>
> So I can wait with hope. I can in my heart bind together the difficult present with a hopeful future (in this world) of God's involvement and goodness. I can live in light of God.

---

* Judy works for Campus Crusade for Christ in the office of the president (who happens to be her husband—but you only need to spend about three seconds in the vicinity of her wise brain and godly heart to put any charges of nepotism out of your mind).

I will therefore be strong. I will seize and fasten on God and who He is. I will take heart and will bring my emotions, intellect, and will under His loving sovereignty.

I will eagerly anticipate what God will do. I will wait with hope.[38]

I love that. How great is David's choosing to "bind together the difficult present with a hopeful future" in his heart? How great would it be for us to do the same thing—to take the present garbage and bind it to a hopeful future? Wonderful!

In fact, it reminds me (and this is going to be odd) of something I do with my kids when they get hurt. Actually, many Spanish-speaking people do it (this Swede can't take credit for a Latin culture!). I learned it from my husband, who learned it from his mom and aunt who learned it from their mom and so on.

Anyway, when one of my kids gets hurt, they want a little *sana*, which means, they want me to rub their ow-ee and say, "*Sana, sana, culito de rana. Si no sanas hoy, sanarás mañana.*" And then I kiss their boo-boo.

For the longest time I was afraid to ask *what* this meant (let's just say more than a couple of witchcrafty things have snuck into even the most God-fearing Cuban households), but it turns out the phrase translates to, "Heal, heal, little frog's butt. If you don't heal today, you'll heal tomorrow." Cute, huh?

So this reminds me of David, because as my kids watch me do the *sana*, they fully expect to feel better. They choose to believe it's going to work. That Mama can make it better. Even though each of them has had plenty of experience with it not working right away. But, of course, since they speak Spanish, they get that last little bit—the part about if the frog's butt doesn't heal today, well, then tomorrow.

That's hope, people. That's the choice. "If not today, then tomorrow." We may need to say this every single morning, noon, and night, but that's how we stand on the promise. It's not easy, but it's lovely.

Believe One, Believe Them All

And then there's this bit about promises, which my friend Charlotte reminded me of one day when she messaged me this: "Heaven, eternity, the truths of the gospel, the hugeness of God's love for us, his sovereignty. . . . If all of that isn't real, if he isn't in this with me, then what's the point? My ultimate hope HAS to be in him, or I seriously couldn't handle this life."

That's hope, people. That's the choice. "If not today, then tomorrow."

Charlotte's onto something here— there's not much to hold on to if our hope is not in him. But it was the six little words "if all of that isn't real" that got to me. Because I realize how silly I've been about these promises. We can't be selective about *which* promises we believe. If we believe one, we must believe them all. If we believe he won't send world-destroying floods, we need to believe our plans will succeed in him. If we believe he made a great nation, we need to believe he can prosper us. If we believe God sent his Son and is preparing an everlasting Kingdom, we need to believe that when we ask, we'll receive; that when we seek, we'll find; and that when we knock, the door will swing open, that our God will welcome us in off the stoop.

In an e-mail from a colleague who had recently suffered all sorts of personal trauma—including a flood that destroyed the lower level of her home—I read:

I was alone at the table in my son's kitchen. My personal floodgates opened, and I experienced a sense of despair like none I'd ever felt before. I begged God for something, anything, to help me pull it together and do what needed to be done.

He took me to 1 Peter 1:3-9: "Praise be to the God and Father of our Lord Jesus Christ. In his great mercy he has given us new birth into a living hope through the resurrection of Jesus Christ from the dead, and into an inheritance that can never perish, spoil, or fade—kept in heaven for you who through faith are shielded by God's power until the coming of the salvation that is ready to be revealed in the last time. In this you greatly rejoice, though now for a little while you may have had to suffer grief in all kinds of trials. These have come so that your faith—of greater worth than gold, which perishes even though refined by fire—may be proved genuine and may result in praise, glory, and honor when Jesus Christ is revealed. Though you have not seen him, you love him; and even though you do not see him now, you believe in him and are filled with an inexpressible and glorious joy, for you are receiving the goal of your faith, the salvation of your souls."

I'm never happy when friends, family, or colleagues suffer, but I'm always thrilled when they share what God has shown them in their suffering—how he has lifted them out and changed them through it. This time was no exception. My colleague had no idea that by sharing this passage with me she was offering me a blessing and in fact delivering a reassuring message from God I had longed for. She didn't know that when I asked God why he made it so hard to stand on his promises, he'd use her e-mail to answer my question and bolster my own faith.

She didn't know that when I asked God why he made it so hard to stand on his promises, he'd use her e-mail to answer my question and bolster my own faith.

This passage in 1 Peter says the Lord allows the grief and the trials to refine our faith and to glorify Jesus. In fact, it is through our day-to-day hope and expectancy for God to show up and do mighty things in us and through us that we not only glorify Jesus but let others see him through us. Which is exactly what we're going to talk about next. I hope.

OKAY, GOD:

I'm really having trouble believing your promises today. I'm having a hard time believing you are faithful. Maybe even that you are good. I'm losing hope. And I don't want to. Help me hope. Help me to wait in you. And wait. With you. Yes, this is so hard—help me rest on the promise that you are using what I never would have wanted to make me more like you.

Anyhow, God, Hallelujah.

Amen.

Getting to Hallelujah

Questions for Reflection and Discussion

1. What are some of the promises of God that you find easy to believe? Why?

2. Which ones do you find difficult to accept? Why?

3. Which life experiences most shape the "believability" factor of God's promises for you?

4. What are some promises of God you've seen lived out?

5. Which ones are you waiting on right now?

6. What is your frame of mind, generally, during waiting seasons? Are you patient? anxious? hopeful? pessimistic?

PART V

Flash Your Hallelujah

CHAPTER 13

LIVE FREE

Letting Go of the Chains That Hold You Down

AFTER TELLING A FRIEND about my "theories" about being stuck in life (see chapter 4), she tilted her head, squinted one eye, and said, "Huh." Then she clucked her tongue twice.

"What?" I asked. "Am I wrong?"

"No," she said. (Though, would I tell you if she said yes—thereby admitting that reading chapter 4 had been a complete waste of your time? Probably not.) "It's just that I think I feel less *stuck* in life and more *weighed down.*"

She went on to explain how she felt like she actually moved forward through life. She made progress. She could every now and again stop on whatever path she was on, turn around, and take a gander back from whence she'd come.

The trouble was, she said, she felt so *burdened.* Though she progressed through life, she was too exhausted to enjoy any of the "tethered and heavy" steps of her journey. And by the time she got anywhere, she was just too worn-out and sore to appreciate how far she'd come or look forward to where she was going.

"That," she said, "is what I hate about my life."

My mind immediately went to motherhood. I've said it before and I'll say it a zillion times again, I'm sure: I love being a mom. I love my kids. But for all the love and snuggles and laughs and proud moments, kids have a way of weighing you down—figuratively and literally. Let's just say I get a lot more done when the kids are at school.

When I brought this up, my friend agreed but said that wasn't really it. She meant more all the other stuff of life. The stuff she feels sort of pressured into. The stuff at church. The stuff at school. (See? It *is* the kids!) The *obligations* of life.

As it turned out, because of our various weighty obligations, we couldn't continue the conversation, but her words stayed with me. I couldn't shake what she had said. I started an inventory of my life and its "obligations."

Honestly, I'm running pretty thin right now. My big obligations include: taking care of my kids, paying some attention to my husband, finishing the writing and editing jobs that bring home some bacon, serving on a school board, and being on a worship-planning committee at church, all while attempting to keep the house somewhat decent.

Except for the housework one, while each of these obligations certainly keeps me hopping, none seems like a burdensome obligation. None of them makes me feel "tethered" or "weighed down." Each of them, even when frustrating or stressful, has its own reward.

So I thought back further—to former obligations in my life—and started noticing that I felt worn-out just by *remembering* some of my past obligations (my year of helping preschoolers at the Play-Doh table comes to mind here). As I thought about some of the stuff that used to be in my life, I sort of shuddered at the role they played and then rejoiced at their absence.

Then I realized something. I had, somewhere along the way, gotten good at saying "no" to the stuff I just didn't want to do. Though I am by nature a people pleaser and someone for whom the words *new* and *opportunity* lead to a racing heart and broad smile, I can turn down an invitation or an opportunity without a second thought. I've gotten good at discerning whether something will energize me or burden me, and I try to fill my life with the things that energize me. Because after all the living dead stuff we talked about, I know those are the things that God made me to do—mostly, anyway.

Though it wasn't always this way.

Back When I Was Burdened

You can get the whole crazy scoop on the onslaught of my years-long motherhood-induced identity crisis in my first book, *Mama's Got a Fake I.D.* While that predated my "I hate my life" crisis (my thirties have been such a treat!) by a good couple of years, the overlap between them helped "cure" my identity crisis.

Funny how that works. I learned that when you're hunkered down, doing battle with life and the world, you've got to figure out pretty quick who you are and what you can do to survive.

Because when life had been "rosy," I had gotten myself mixed up into a bunch of stuff that drained me: volunteering for things I hated; hanging with people who, while I didn't *hate* them by any stretch, definitely didn't "get" me, and vice versa; and saying yes to any old bit of work or volunteer opportunity that came my way for fear of never being asked again and drifting into oblivion.

I was burdened by obligations and people that had no business being in my life. But I didn't know how to say no—and I was scared of how I'd look (e.g., lazy, insensitive, selfish, etc.) if I did.

Here's where God got good. The thing is, when you have to earn money to feed your kids, to pay for their vaccines, to cover their heads, it gets a whole lot easier to say no to things that might get in the way of that.

When you feel your marriage cracking under the stresses of life, it's a whole lot easier to say no to things that lump cement and pile bricks on top of that stress.

And when you feel your own mind slipping; when you've lain, curled up, on a cold and sticky kitchen floor, crying about your pit of a life, you get particular about what you can do and who you want to do it with.

Frankly, this whole spell left me with so little energy and so few resources that I had only God to turn to. (Praise God for this. If only this was the way we *always* felt.) It was his way or the I-don't-even-want-to-think-about-it way.

As I sought God and his guidance and his provision, I felt him turning it right back to me. Not to get all New Age-y and not meaning to be all "just look inside yourself" about it, but really, the answer I got from God was that he'd given me tools. He'd given me gifts. And he'd given me the people I needed in my life to help me manage.

I had just buried those resources under all the other garbage and time wasters I was letting into my life. I needed to come out from under that rubble. I needed to start saying no.

Here's where the collision between my identity crisis and my "I hate my life" crisis happened: to unburden my life and figure out what I needed to rid my life of, I had to figure out who I was and what I was made to do.

Clearly, since I had been given children, I was made to be a mom (whether I thought I was particularly "gifted" at it or not). But that was just the start. I began to look at my other gifts. I had to look at my spiritual gifts (which for me are giving, encouragement, and creative ability), and I had to look at my talents and abilities. I had to look at what I loved to do, what fired me up, what made a day great. I had to figure out what I could do well that not everybody else could. What energized me—but maybe felt burdensome to others.

I had to figure out the answer to Frederick Buechner's famous quote on vocation: If "the place where God calls you to is the place where your deep gladness and the world's deep needs meet," then what was mine?

What is yours?

I e-mailed the friend who felt weighed down to ask her if maybe she had too many things she hated to do in her life— and if maybe she could get rid of a few.

She wrote back that she'd been thinking the same thing. And that really, it was just one thing. *One* thing that caused her to feel like she was slouching along in her journey through life—tugging that old ball and chain. She had talked to her husband about it and decided she'd finish out her commitment to the one icky thing and then "be free!"

She was excited to see if her pace would pick up, she said. To see how it felt to walk a little lighter. If her stride would lengthen, maybe.

The Race We're Called to Run

Again, I need to write a quick disclaimer, because the last thing I want you to take from all this is that God only wants us to say yes to the things of life that are easy, that bring smiles to our faces, and that fill us with constant joy.

I'm not saying that God only wants us to say yes to the things of life that are easy, that bring smiles to our faces, and that fill us with constant joy.

That is a lie. And we need to get that right out of our heads. The easiest example I can come up with (and I use this one frequently) is church nursery. I am not now nor ever have been particularly "gifted" with babies or small children. I'm great with my own—and I'm *nice* to kids, trust me—but I'm certainly not energized by them. They scare me a little. I feel clueless.

An hour of nursery duty on a Sunday morning leaves me exhausted and desperate. In fact, the day—the day!—my youngest son turned three and therefore "graduated" from church nursery, I announced to my husband, "Praise the Lord! We never have to volunteer for the nursery again."

Because, in theory, I had volunteered to help out only because of an obligation. Parents of children who use the nursery—rightfully so—are encouraged to fill out a background-check form and volunteer to help out in the nursery once a quarter or so.

While these precious four hours a year nearly kill me, they also meet one of the great ministry needs of our church. One of our pastors recently told me that something like 50 percent of the visitors who come back to our church the following week do so because of the *nursery*. Can you imagine how painful that is for a preacher to admit?

What I'm saying is that we are sometimes asked— obliged, even—to do things for God that don't tickle the fancy bone, if you will. We're told to give, to share—and not just when it's easy or fun. We're told to care for widows and orphans—and not just if we're "good" at it. We're told to *love our enemies*, for goodness' sake. And that's never easy and rarely energizing.

Beyond the sweeping biblical callings, each of us will come across things that just need doing and we end up being the person to do them—simply because we're able and in the right place at the right time.

We don't have an excuse to say no to some of the needs of this world simply because we don't *feel* like doing them. If the Spirit so moves us when we pass a hungry person on the street, we can't just pass her by because we're not "gifted" in giving. Following Jesus doesn't work like that.

That said, Jesus didn't heal everybody while he was on earth. Jesus didn't leave every last poor person with pockets full of coins. He didn't do "everything" while he was here— and yet he did what he was supposed to, of course. And Jesus was perfect.

So I can't help but believe that God doesn't expect us to take on and tackle every little problem of the world by ourselves. He gives each of us passions and cares and abilities to match the needs of the world. And he expects us to follow the biblical mandates based on those.

Use 'em If You Got 'em

In Luke 12:48, Jesus says, "When someone has been given much, much will be required in return; and when someone has been entrusted with much, even more will be required."

I love this verse—but I think we tend to consider it in terms of *monetary* gifts. But if we apply it to *all* our gifts (which I think we should) it helps us understand what is expected of us. We're to use—well and often—the gifts we're given. If we've been given smarts, we're supposed to use them. If we've been given humor, we've got to use that. If we've been given the ability to make a killer loaf of bread, God expects us to use it.

When we find ourselves stumbling along, struggling because our days are filled with tasks and events that don't use any of our gifts, we need to take a hard look at why we're doing them.

So I think this is a great way to look at what exactly we're supposed to fill our days and our lives with. When we find ourselves stumbling along, struggling because our days are filled with tasks and events that don't use any of our gifts, we need to take a hard look at why we're doing them. Out of guilt? Because we feel too bad saying no? Because everybody else is doing it? Because our church, our community, or our families simply *expect* us to?

We have to lay those things down before God—like we

talked about in the "Live Dead" chapter. We have to ask God what he expects from us—if he wants us doing the things that don't seem to line up with how he made us or who he made us to be. Then we have to ask—and expect—that if God wants us to continue serving in this place or in this way, he'll resurrect it in such a way that it fits or uses our gifts more and that God will give us a glimpse of why it matters to him.

Learning that the number one reason visitors returned for a second Sunday was our nursery humbled me—and my view of nursery duty. While I viewed it as an hour or so of me wiping the tears, noses, and bottoms of children not my own, I'm guessing God sees it differently. He sees it as a spot that allows people (the kids and their parents) to feel welcomed and embraced in his house. Which is a burden that God has placed on my heart too.

Mind you, I don't feel called to put my name back on the nursery list, but learning to see how God probably views this ministry helps me remember that sometimes we will be asked to do things for God that might not perfectly fit our gifts. And we should step up when a need arises.

However, if we're stepping up only out of guilt or false expectations or even security (after all, the same chains that weigh us down also offer a measure of—or the illusion of—safety), we need to let these things go. Most of the times I've done this, I've felt that "peace" about letting things go. Even good things. Even good (and some not-so-good-for-me) people. But finding the courage and willingness to pop the locks on those chains that hold us down frees us to live as we were meant to.

The Race We Were Meant to Run

I'm no runner. In fact, as I mentioned before, running makes my knees hurt, my stomach cramp, and my legs itch. A few times in my life I've tried—*pretended* maybe is the better word—to become a runner, but it just doesn't work. Not my gift. I like riding my bike. I like walking. But running—unless it's from something horrifying or to something wonderful? Forget it.

Naturally, I have a love-hate relationship with Hebrews 12:1-3:

> *Since we are surrounded by such a huge crowd of witnesses to the life of faith, let us strip off every weight that slows us down, especially the sin that so easily trips us up. And let us run with endurance the race God has set before us. We do this by keeping our eyes on Jesus, the champion who initiates and perfects our faith. Because of the joy awaiting him, he endured the cross, disregarding its shame. Now he is seated in the place of honor beside God's throne. Think of all the hostility he endured from sinful people; then you won't become weary and give up.*

I love, love, love the image. I see it in slo-mo, like a commercial. I'm wearing all white, sort of gauzy pants and a matching tunic. I've got gauzy scarves around my neck and I'm peeling them off as I run; they blow off into the wind behind me, landing in the surf that licks at my feet. And I keep running, smiling, while the "huge crowd of witnesses" claps and cheers as I pass by. I'm thinking about what Jesus endured for me, and I'm running toward that throne, which

is at the end of the beach, just beyond the curve, before some
rocks. (It looks a lot like a beach in Malibu I walked along
years ago. Except I'm not worried about those snakes in the
tall grass on the hills.)

And I run, free, toward Jesus. I love that.

It's when I take it out of dream sequence that I start getting nervous. Then the hate part of my relationship with this
verse kicks in. It's when it stops being slow-mo and starts
moving in real time that I panic. It's when I get myself off
that beach and back onto the black, cracked asphalt that I
start wondering if I really can do this, if I can endure. Because
I remember that I hate running. It hurts and makes me suffer.

Suffering. That brings me back to my Jesus. Trudging
along that road, torn, bleeding, being mocked and jeered at
by the crowds. Weighed down by the cross on which he'd
hang. How did he do that? How did he endure the agony?
Not because he was God. I don't believe he
pulled a superhuman card or performed any
miracles on himself so it wouldn't hurt—he
was human enough to feel every throb of
pain. He endured because his eyes were on
God and on "the joy awaiting him."

*Jesus endured
because his eyes
were on God
and on "the joy
awaiting him."*

He did carry what he had to—as should
we, since not everything we're gifted with
or called to do is easy, as I said. After all, Jesus tells us to take
up our own crosses and follow him (see Mark 8:34). It's not
an easy road, necessarily, when we follow Jesus and live the
life, run the race, that's set out for us. But if we want to love
our lives and honor God in doing it, we've got to get rid of all
the nonessentials of life that encumber us, that keep us from

doing what God wants us to do or being what he wants us to be or seeing what he wants us to see. We've got to do this if we want to receive the joy that's promised.

Of course, this passage in Hebrews isn't talking only about the annoying extra tasks of life that weigh us down. It's "especially" the sin that weighs us down that we need to address. To rid ourselves of. To be forgiven for. If we want to run (or walk, hike, skip, or twirl!) our races well, with our eyes fixed on Jesus and the joy that awaits us, we need to be free from the shackles of sin.

Since we're broken—permanently—this doesn't mean we need to never sin. That's impossible. We will sin. This is not to say, of course, that we should go out of our way to pull some doozies, to see how many commandments we can break in one sitting or anything. However, when we do find ourselves sinning—or having sinned—we need to repent and accept the grace, mercy, forgiveness for which Jesus suffered. We need to accept the gift that *his* "race" here on earth was all about.

Again in Hebrews, we're told: "See to it that no one falls short of the grace of God and that no bitter root grows up to cause trouble" (Hebrews 12:15, NIV). I love the image of a bitter root growing *up* and causing trouble— especially in light of the running the race talk. Roots can either grow up to entangle us or to trip us—either way, they hold us back during our race, make it hurt much more than it should.

Jesus tells us that in this world we will have trials. We know that. But since Jesus came to free us from the tangles of sin and to free us from the burdens of intricate rules and regulations, we can trust that he wants us to keep our focus on him—and on his purpose for us. If something isn't a good use of our time, if someone isn't a healthy companion for us, if something in our lives causes us so much stress or exhaustion that we can't do what we're meant to do, we need to find freedom from that.

I'm not saying God wants us to ship our kids off to boarding school; give our difficult marriages the old heave-ho; drop that dog at the shelter; and quit teaching Sunday school midyear, leaving the kids high and dry with nary a filmstrip. *Au contraire.* We're to honor commitments. We're to be honest and faithful.

But since Jesus came to free us from the tangles of sin and to free us from the burdens of intricate rules and regulations, we can trust that he wants us to keep our focus on him—and on his purpose for us.

But even within commitments, we have room to untether ourselves. To wriggle out from under undue burdens. To free up our stride so we can really run this race well. Even good things—done wrong or too much—can weigh us down.

But obligations and *sin* aren't the only things that do this. Let's take freedom a step further and look at living naked in the next chapter.

OKAY, GOD:

I'm tired. I feel overburdened and overwhelmed. I've said yes to too many things and need a break. Help me know what I should be doing—what you want me to do. Thank you that you've never expected me—never even wanted me—to do everything. And help me let go of the things that are holding me back. Thank you that I no longer need to live as a slave to the sin that once separated me from you.

Anyhow, God, Hallelujah.

Amen.

Getting to Hallelujah
Questions for Reflection and Discussion

1. When you envision yourself running the race as described in Hebrews, what do you imagine?

2. What sorts of things in your life trip you up in that race?

3. What are some of the things you've been saying yes to only out of guilt or a false sense of obligation? Do you really need to continue doing them?

4. How might your life improve if you learned to say no more often?

5. What things might you say no to so you can be freed up to say yes to more important things? What are those priorities for which you want to make more room in your life?

CHAPTER 14

LIVE NAKED

Letting Go of Shame

I CAN STILL FEEL the churning in my stomach and the swirl-ing in head as I plodded up the cement stairs into church the Sunday morning after my parents told me that my dad was moving out. I can still feel my palms, sweaty and slippery, as I tightly gripped my newborn daughter's infant carrier.

I hated walking into this place where I knew that soon enough my family would become fodder for gossip—like I'd heard so many other families gossiped about before.* I hated that now church would be a place where people would stare and whisper, where I'd have to field questions I didn't want to answer and face things I didn't want to face.

Had I not gone to the same church I grew up in—the one my parents were still members of (though not attendees)—none of this would have been an issue, of course, but it was. My

---

*Please understand: I don't belong to an especially gossipy church. I'd hate for you to imagine a bunch of harpies standing at the doors, pointing and whispering just before throwing on fake smiles and waving hello. It's not like that at all. But I do go to a *human* church. And people do gossip.

family had gone to this church for more than twenty-five years at that point. My family's relative longevity there was one of the reasons I still belonged to that church—I liked the rootedness. I had dreamed of being one of those families that stretches across an entire pew. Not because I had a pew full of kids, mind you, but because three generations would sit together, passing candy and shushing. I thought that would be great.

But with news of my dad moving out and divorce attorneys being called, that little bubble got burst in a hurry. That pew dream was over. So with shame and embarrassment and scorched dreams, I went to church. I didn't hear the sermon. I didn't sing the songs. I just sat—or stood. Smiled at my husband when he took our older son down to nursery. And sat again, until I had to take my crying daughter out.

That's where I ran into my friend "Mary." Mary had noticed my daze during the service and came out to see if I was okay.

I faced a choice: either I could pull it together and smile and say, "Of course! I'm fine. Just a little tired." I was the mother of a two-year-old and a one-month-old. I had a good excuse.

Or I could tell her the truth.

I remember taking a deep breath, hugging my daughter tighter, and risking the truth. I told her about my parents. About how sad I was. About how embarrassed I was. About how afraid I was of hearing people gossip about my family.

I vaguely remember Mary putting a hand on my arm and saying she was sorry or something, but then it gets clear. "My parents are married only technically," she said. "They live separate, horrible lives. They hate each other."

Then she smiled at me. I smiled back and thanked her for sharing that with me. Told her it made me feel less alone.

Then she hugged me and told me not to be embarrassed. And that I certainly wasn't alone. "This place is crawling with husbands and wives who hate each other," she half joked. As we laughed, she encouraged me not to feel as though I needed to hide my parents' news. I didn't need to broadcast it, she said, but just to be real about it. Honest. The gossipers were guilty of worse sins than divorce, she said. And stepping out from my shame, she said, would "free" me.

How right she was. While Satan had succeeded that morning in ruining church by convincing me that now I would be scorned and humiliated and unloved and unwelcomed, God sent Mary to show me the bigger truth.

We are better when we're willing to walk through life naked, showing scars, showing brokenness, showing vulnerability, showing how what we have lived through has made us who we are.

Her words to me were a gift that spared me more time locked in secrecy and shame and that helped me realize that slipping off that shame or shimmying out of those secrets not only frees us and helps us not feel so alone, but it's actually a gift—a ministry, even!—to others.

We are better when we're willing to walk through life naked, showing scars, showing brokenness, showing vulnerability, showing how what we have lived through has made us who we are. And better yet, who God is.

But naked is not easy. Except for in Eden, it never has been.

217

Exposed

In the weeks that followed—as my dad moved out, as the news spread that my parents were separating, as I began to lash out in anger and grief over what it meant for me and my own little family—I realized another part of all this that I hated so much: being exposed.

Following Mary's advice, I began to tell friends—call them up, even—to tell them about my parents. For the most part, I got sympathy. Sometimes I got humor. My favorite response to me saying "My dad moved out" was "Oh! My dad would *love* that!" Again, it was great to laugh and not feel so alone.

Many people responded with shock. "Your parents were like the *perfect* couple." "They *looked* so happy." "But they had a *great* life together."

Of course, as the daughter, I wasn't quite as shocked by the news of my parents' separation as everyone else was. I had always seen behind the carefully constructed facades; I knew what was illusion and what was real.

As those facades began to crumble and the illusions slipped away—leaving my family and our "shame" exposed for all to see—I realized how comforted and protected I had been by those illusions. Even as I talked a big game in my life about needing to "be real," I perpetuated an image of my family that—while not totally false (I grew up in a pretty good home)—covered up a lot. I wanted others to believe my family was as happy as everyone else's *looked.*

It was so stupid. So fruitless. So counter to the way God calls us to live, which is in truth and in love.

While I never asked or wanted the smoke and mirrors

of my family life to be jerked away, once they were, once I had no choice but to walk through life naked and exposed, I learned quickly that this really is the freest way to live. And a great way to learn to love what you've got out there.

Nudist

Because I am Mom of the Year, I let my eight-year-old watch a documentary about a nudist colony with me. Don't freak: it was on PBS, I think. They didn't *show* any nudity. Just nudists in their trailers or cabins. Or at picnics, playing volleyball, always with convenient black bars blocking anything "inappropriate."

Naturally, my son became obsessed with nudists. Even though it's been months since we watched the documentary, he'll still come up to me with a random question about their way of life:

"Do they go into grocery stores naked?"

"What about bugs?"

"Do they sit in their own chairs? Or do they actually borrow other people's?"

I try to answer as best I can, but usually I respond with, "Hey, bud. You watched the same show I did. You know as much about it as I do."

But honestly, I kind of share his preoccupation. I have no—zero—desire to become a nudist. No longing to go to a nude beach, even. Skinny-dipping holds no appeal. (Even alone. I share my son's concern about the bugs. Add fish to that and you get why skinny-dipping doesn't do it for me.)

Yet I'm fascinated that people exist who can ignore the oldest form of shame—nudity! So one night I nervously

Googled *nudism*. Don't worry, this was long after the kids went to bed. I may let them watch documentaries, but I know better than to let them see a Wikipedia site on nudists! I'd caution you to stay away too. That picture of naked badminton has yet to leave my brain.

But I digress: I Googled it because I couldn't shake my questions of why and how people would choose this lifestyle. And I couldn't remember the answer from that documentary. I wanted to know how it could be that Adam and Eve covered up because they were naked and ashamed and yet some people choose to disrobe and go about life that way.

I discovered that many "levels" of nudism exist—as do many terms, though *nudist* is the most fun to type and say, so I'm going with that. But the most interesting part of it to me is the philosophy behind nudism. What amused (and slightly terrified) me is that I agree with a lot of what they stand for—care for the environment, care for animals, equality, respect for other opinions, health, freedom. It's just that I like to care about all those things while wearing clothes.

But while reading a "nondefinitive" and apparently debated list of nudist ideals created by French philosopher and psychologist Marc-Alain Descamps, I was struck by one line in particular: "Rapport with other humans—equality and respect. An anti-war, pro-world government stance."

While, in fact, I'm not a pro-world government kind of gal (see, I disagree with nudists on plenty of things too), I read this and thought, *Of course they'd have great rapport with others. Of course you'd be a pacifist if you walked around nude!*

Now maybe this is naive, but it seems if you've committed to living *naked*, you've also sort of waved the white flag of physical competition. Sure, some people have naturally "better" or more culturally appealing physiques than others. But I'd think that a commitment to nudity equals a commitment to showing your physical beauty and flaws to the world—without "help" from clothes that boost or cinch, from colors that bring out your eyes or draw attention to your cheeks (the ones on your face, that is), or stripes that pull eyes up and away from trouble spots.

This sort of "freedom" would seem to allow for greater rapport. For a better sense of "equality." For a broader ability to listen to other people's opinions. It would be much harder to think "war" while nude.

After all, you could see each other's flaws—the scars, the flab, the puckers of cellulite, the rashes, and the scabs. With all that vulnerability, of course you'd have greater understanding for the people around you. When you've known how terrifying it is to step out under the clear blue sky wearing nothing but your aging and sagging birthday suit, no doubt you are going to look a little more gently on those who step out beside you.

Still, I don't want to be a nudist. I don't want to hang out with nudists, quite frankly. At least, not physical nudists. But I do want to be a sort of emotional, maybe spiritual, nudist. I want to hang out with those kind too.

Because being exposed, living naked, and being vulnerable opens your heart. It helps you understand. It's a lot harder to be harsh with others—be merciless, as we talked about in chapter 9—when you're standing there, with scars or even fresh wounds visible for the world to see. It's hard to ignore other people's pain and shame when you know you've walked around with yours exposed as well.

Be Nude, Not Pornographic

This spring I heard Parker Palmer speak at Calvin College's Festival of Faith and Writing. I filled two solid legal-pad pages of notes from his talk, it was that good. While my favorite line of his talk was, "I became a writer because I was born baffled" (true for most of us writers), my favorite *part* was when he warned us about when the "soul story becomes schtick."[39]

Parker talked about the difficulties of sharing the truth of our stories without baring every last detail. He talked about the dilemma in trying to make a "soul connection" with readers. Do you tell the whole story? Do you hint at details? Do you preserve anything for yourself?

"Writing is public therapy," Parker said. "But some should stay private."

As I've written this book, I've taken those words to heart. And, frankly, when it comes to living naked, I think we should take this to heart as well.

Now, Caryn, you may be thinking, *you just said we should live naked, exposed!*

Yes, I did. And I still think that living without shame and being willing to show our scars and our imperfections (as well as our good parts!) is the best way to live. But walking around naked still doesn't mean showing "everything."

It's the difference, I think, between living naked and being pornographic. Right? A naked body is a beautiful work of art, a creation of God. But we can twist it (literally or figuratively) and make it *too* exposed. Then it becomes a dangerous thing.

So it is with emotional nudism. We can tell our stories and share our hurts, our dreams, and our disappointments without sharing every last detail. I can tell you that my parents are divorced, that my marriage has hit hard times, and that our finances are a mess without giving details that, frankly, aren't even entirely mine to give.

I don't spare them because I'm ashamed but because they are private. The details of some of the events and circumstances of my life are reserved for only a select few. In the way that my body is, actually. Showing everything—allowing true intimacy—is not an option I want to give to the masses.

We can tell our stories and share our hurts, our dreams, and our disappointments without sharing every last detail.

So even as I say that living naked brings freedom, it may also threaten our safety at times. This means that we do need to be mindful of whom and what and where we tell. Not everyone needs full stories. Not everyone deserves all the details.

Being an emotional nudist frees *you* to live as the person God made you to be. It's what allows you to show off the stories of God's faithfulness and goodness. Of how he's taken hurt and pain, tragedy and disappointment, and given you a new life and freedom. Of how he's using you—your good parts and redeemed crummy parts—to transform this world. To be a light in it.

When my friend Mary opened up about her own family's brokenness, she was a light in my darkness. She showed me the power of openness and honesty without betraying her family or giving too many details. She showed me I wasn't alone and shouldn't be ashamed. And frankly, she opened my eyes to all the hurting families around me at church.

Where before all I could see were the "perfect" families

that plopped three generations of butts across a pew, now I realized how many broken, hurting families there were. How many single moms. How many troubled kids. How many unfaithful husbands and wives. How many addicts. How many abusers. How many abused. How many lonely, hurting, broken people. In fact, not one person in those pews wasn't hurting or lonely or broken in some way.

And as I began to walk around more exposed about other areas of my life—our marriage, our finances—and therefore look around my church and community through my other filters of what I was exposing, I saw the people around me change too.

Suddenly not everyone was richer than I was. Not everyone was "luckier" than me. Everyone had troubles. Exposing my flaws made me more aware of those around me. Not so I could judge or feel aloof, but so I could sympathize, be understanding, show mercy.

I once heard songwriter Steve Earle say, in a documentary on Johnny Cash's life, that you "become a tolerant human being by becoming too aware of your own shortcomings."[40] That made me sit up and listen. He went on to say that it wasn't only Johnny's awareness of his shortcomings that made him great (and tolerant of others), but that it was his willingness to live in the "contradictions of his own darkness and light."

I think that's what living naked is all about. It's more than giving every sordid detail. It's a willingness to let others see us weak (our darkness) so that they can see God's strength (his light in us). But it's also about being willing to share the bad, hard stuff of our lives so that when we do share the good stuff (and each of us has plenty of good), it doesn't come off as braggadocio or insincere. Showing both the bad and the good allows others to see us more fully. More completely. More how we're meant to be seen.

In a post for childless women on Mother's Day, one of my all-time favorite writers, Vinita Hampton Wright, rightly writes,[*] "So, as best you can this Mother's Day, allow your desire for giving life to beat wildly and without shame. When words come to the surface—words of pain, anxiety, anger, anticipation, longing, joy—share them somehow, with someone. If you stay silent, the world will suffer for it. If you hide your life because it wasn't the one you'd hoped for, the human family will miss you, and grieve."[41]

I love that. Yes, indeed, when we don't tell our stories, when we hide our hurts and disappointments, we hide who we are, and the human family—and, yes, the Kingdom of God!—misses us and grieves. So we need to show them who we are, to live naked, so the human family can instead rejoice.

But it isn't just other people who benefit from our willingness to be vulnerable and share our scars and sufferings—we benefit too. It frees us up and unbinds us from the shackles of shame to live and love the lives that God has in store for us.

I once told my therapist a story about the first time I gave an acquaintance a peek into

A willingness to let others see us weak allows them to see God's strength. And if we share the bad, hard stuff of our lives, when we share the good stuff (and each of us has plenty of good), it doesn't come off as braggadocio or insincere.

---

[*] Sorry. I'm a sucker for homonyms.

the effects of depression's dark cloud on my home. I didn't give this acquaintance all the details, but I hinted clearly at what was going on. I told my therapist that even my dropping hints, even giving this woman a peek at what lay beneath the roof and between the walls of my home, made me feel like I was "lifting the veil" on my life. And it felt so good. Those fresh breezes blowing on my face felt like freedom. The clarity with which my eyes now saw felt like hope.

When we hide who we are, the human family misses us and grieves.

My therapist smiled as I said this. Yes, that's the freedom and hope Jesus came for, my therapist told me. Jesus didn't want us to be tangled in shame; he wanted us to be free in him, he said.

I love the way *The Message* translates Galatians 5:1: "Christ has set us free to live a free life. So take your stand! Never again let anyone put a harness of slavery on you."

We have choices. We can sit back and let secrets and shame be that harness of slavery; we can let our lives stay veiled, concealed under our own imposed burkas—convinced that it's safer and better for us. Or we can accept the freedom that Christ offers. To lay our shame and secrets at his feet, to look to him for their redemption, and to allow those very things we want to hide become the funnel, the vessel, the window through which Jesus' light shines.

OKAY, GOD:

You know I've got a lot to be ashamed of. I may have your comfort and your grace, but I'm not so sure of everybody else's. And yet, I'm so sick and tired of working so hard to

cover my shame. Will you please just take my shame away?
And will you help me be proud to show the work you've done
in me? I don't know how you do it, but I thank you that you can
transform even the ugliest parts of my past into a sign of your
glory and grace.

Anyhow, God, Hallelujah.

Amen.

Getting to Hallelujah
Questions for Reflection and Discussion

1. What sorts of things do you tend to hide under? What are
   the shameful things or secrets that keep you from loving
   your life?

2. What might being free from those look or feel like?

3. How would you describe the difference between living
   naked and living "pornographic"? Does this distinction
   help or hinder your understanding of what living free
   from shame can be like?

4. Do your secrets feel like a harness of slavery to you?
   How so?

CHAPTER 15

LIVE SALTY AND SHINY

Letting Go of the Dark and the Drab

AFTER DROPPING MY KIDS OFF at school, I flipped on *Midday Connection*, a nationally syndicated Christian radio show hosted by Anita Lustrea and Melinda Schmidt. That day they had author and speaker Trish Berg on. I caught the show *in medias res*, so I didn't know what they were talking about. It didn't even matter to me what came before or after once I heard what Trish was saying.

One day, Trish said, she had seen a barn full of cracks and holes, with light streaming through each and every one of them. We should be like the barn siding, Trish said—not generating our own light, but allowing God's light to shine through our imperfections.

I don't remember what exactly was going on in my life that day, but I pulled over immediately after I heard this so I could jot it down. As I fumbled for a pen and paper, the tears started. They continued as I summarized what I'd just heard. It took several minutes before I could see well enough to drive again.

While I don't remember the specifics of what caused those tears, I know I heard this during a season where the difficulties of my life had made me hard. Bitter. Angry. Resentful. Calloused. Ugly.

No light was getting through my imperfections because I had plugged those holes right up—sloppily but soundly—so that no one could see in and certainly no light could come out. But in the car, in that moment, I knew that had to change.

"This Little Light of Mine" came to mind as I pictured what my caulked-up-barn-of-a-life was doing to the light inside me. I was hiding it under a bushel. Yes! I was failing Basic Jesus Living 101. All because I was hurt. All because I was scared. All because I was angry. All because I felt alone. And yet by closing myself off, I was keeping myself trapped in a place of even more pain.

The Well-Lit Life

When I got back home, I looked up all the verses about light in Scripture. Turns out, there are lots and lots (and lots!) of verses about light. So then I narrowed them down to what Jesus had to say about light. I went straight for the "salt and light" passages, but stopped first at the Beatitudes, which directly precede them.

During my reading, something new struck me. See if you notice what stuck out. (Note: It's a long passage, and I know we all like to skim over Scripture in books [I'm human too], but please bear with me.)

God blesses *those who are* poor *and* realize their need *for him,*
  for the Kingdom of Heaven is theirs.
God blesses *those who* mourn,
  for they will be comforted.
God blesses *those who are* humble,
  for they will inherit the whole earth.
God blesses *those who* hunger *and* thirst *for justice,*
  for they will be satisfied.
God blesses *those who are* merciful,
  for they will be shown mercy.
God blesses *those whose hearts are* pure,
  for they will see God.
God blesses *those who* work for peace,
  for they will be called the children of God.
God blesses *those who are* persecuted *for doing right,*
  for the Kingdom of Heaven is theirs.

God blesses *you* when people mock *you and* persecute *you*
and lie *about you and say all sorts of evil things against you*
because you are my followers. . . .

You *are the* salt *of the earth. . . .*

You *are the* light *of the world.*
(Matthew 5:3-11, 13-14, emphasis mine)

Notice anything? Did my emphasized hints help?

Well, here's what got me: While we normally read the
Sermon on the Mount all chunked up into handy sections,
I'm not sure Jesus offered a session break at the end of the
Beatitudes. I doubt he sent people off for fish and wine and

a few minutes of networking. Nope, I'd venture to guess Jesus went straight from the "God blesses" into the salt and light bit—and that has to mean something. It can't be coincidence that just after Jesus says that God *blesses* people who hurt and grieve and are mocked, he says, "*You* are the salt of the earth" and then "*You* are the light of the world."

It seems to be broken, hurting—but caring and kind—people who are the salt and light.

It seems to be broken, hurting—but caring and kind—people who are the salt and light. They are the ones who bring out the flavor from the bland, who shine in the darkness of this world. It's the people who have known suffering who do this. The people whose light shines through the cracks and holes in their own siding.

The salt and light passage wraps up with this: "No one lights a lamp and then puts it under a basket. Instead, a lamp is placed on a stand, where it gives light to everyone in the house. In the same way, let your good deeds shine out for all to see, so that everyone will praise your heavenly Father" (Matthew 5:15-16).

While, of course, this light comes from God in the first place, it's in our "good deeds" that people see this light. It's what we do that allows it to shine through our imperfections. It's how we live that allows others to see God at work in us.

Light from the Darkness

For the past several years—during this season of grumbling my hallelujahs—one of my favorite hymns has been "Turn Your Eyes upon Jesus." For a while, I seriously wanted to frame the chorus and hang it above my mantel. The words are lovely:

Turn your eyes upon Jesus
Look full in his wonderful face
And the things of earth will grow strangely dim
In the light of his glory and grace.

Or, at least, I *thought* they were lovely until Pastor Gregg ruined them for me. In the middle of a worship-planning/service-brainstorm meeting, I suggested this song—as it would fit in perfectly with the sermon. And then I mentioned how much I loved it.

And Gregg said that he loved it too; although when he was growing up in Grand Rapids, Michigan, it made many of the professors from local Calvin College gruff and huff.

I gasped and asked, "Whatever for?"

Because we're *Reformed*, Gregg said. And Reformed people don't believe things on earth should become "strangely dim" but that they should be illuminated. Transformed.

Aw, shoot. I hated hearing this. What could I do? I'm as Reformed as they come. And these professors—some of whom probably taught *me* at Calvin—were right. We are called to transform the world for Jesus, not to let it all fade away right in front of us.

> *We are called to transform the world for Jesus, not to let it all fade away right in front of us.*

So I tried to hate the song. I really did.

But the trouble is, I still love it. I get a little weak-kneed when I hear and sing it. I still think it *means* something and contains a powerful truth.

Because when I was lost in disappointment and hurt over this life, much of it had to do with *things*—as we've talked about. Physical things and expectation "things." Or ideas, maybe is better. That song healed me in the sense that even when I managed to grumble my hallelujahs, I had a hard time seeing any light—let alone generating or allowing light to pass through the holes and cracks so that it could illuminate the world with Jesus' light.

I needed to focus on Jesus and *find* that light. I needed to see it and absorb the brightness. Get that Jesus vitamin D. Sort of. I needed to lose myself for a while in his light, letting all else grow dim as his light blinded me to the broken world. It was part of the grieving process we talked about in the beginning of this book.

So I kept singing the song. Though, strangely, only the chorus. I never even knew there was a first verse. I stumbled upon it when I Googled it—so I could find a way to print it up fancy and hang it up. I never did print it up because I got lost in discovering the "secret" first verse. It goes like this:

> *O soul, are you weary and troubled?*
> *No light in the darkness you see?*
> *There's a light for a look at the Savior*
> *And life more abundant and free!*

Yes! Looking at the Savior, being in his light, can blind us to the things of earth for a while, but it ultimately shows us a more free and abundant life.

For me, wrapping myself in that light made things better. But after a while, the warmth and coziness of it started to fade, actually. It began feeling almost wrong—probably because I wasn't experiencing either an abundance or freedom of life. As I began to step back a few paces, I found I could still see the light—as well as the things around me. It wasn't that I was stepping away from Jesus, because he steps with us. His Spirit *lives* within us, for crying out loud. He's not going anywhere! But I sort of zoomed out, took in more of the world, and noticed all the darkness. All the places that needed light. That needed Jesus.

Looking at the Savior, being in his light, can blind us to the things of earth for a while, but it ultimately shows us a more free and abundant life.

I realized that it's okay to be sort of greedy with Jesus and the time in his light for a while; however, our calling isn't to hide behind him but to "go." Jesus said this all the time. To people right around him. Go and sin no more. Go and make disciples. Go and prepare.

"Go and do" is how I hear people paraphrase this. Not "stay and be."

Go and Do

Here's the thing that's worried me ever since I started writing this book: Since it's probably going to get shelved with all the other "self-help" books, by the time you get to this point— to the end—it should have helped you in some area, right?

And I hope it has. In every chapter in this book, I've tried to be honest with you about what has turned my life around in the sense that I've gone from hating it to loving it. Mostly.

But no matter what you do or change, your hands remain tied in a big way when it comes to your life: you cannot change the future. You can't force what happens next. So even after you've gone through all these nifty things that can help you love your life, to find some new "supposed to be's," you could still put down this book and the other shoe could drop. Hard and heavy.

You could lose the jealousy, fight the fears, grieve the hurts, change your expectations, and *still* have things happen that hurt so deeply or disappoint so thoroughly that you're back on the kitchen floor, huddled and crying, hating your life.

I thought of this when I finished Shauna Niequist's book *Bittersweet.* The "thesis" of her book is not unlike mine—it contains wonderful little essays about the bitter and the sweet of life. But at the end, after some particularly sweet chapters, she hits readers with some serious bitter. I almost dropped the book when I got there. Not the happy ending we dream of, that we want when we journey with a writer.

It ends in a hard place. With some of the worst losses a person can fathom. I won't tell you what they are. Go buy the book. But by telling this story, she illustrates the power of this salt and light thing. By sharing her heartbreak, she allowed sweet into the bitter, light into the dark.

Though Shauna's book ends with a hard story, in a hard place, in many ways it's the brightest part of the book. The happy ending is that Jesus still reigns, even when life is too hard too bear.

Shauna writes: "I wanted, of course, for this bittersweet season to be over. I felt so strongly that when I finished the book, I'd be free to move into another season, one of life and celebration. But this is what I know now: they're the same thing, and that's all there is. The most bittersweet season of my life so far is still life, still beautiful, still sparkling with celebration."[42]

I love that she uses the word *sparkling* here. Because while living salty and shiny is not always about being happy and festive (as some Christians will tell you), while it's not shimmering jewels and a soothing soak in bath salts, living salty and shiny does celebrate the *all* of life. And we tell it and we show it and we let others be dazzled by the Light of the World—as it streams through our brokenness, as we live our lives as Christ would have us.

Because no matter what we have to endure, what we have to go through, what trials we have to bear in this world, we can take heart because Jesus has overcome the world. While this sounds lofty and romantic, this simply means we cannot lose. We cannot be defeated. And we cannot be beat down because our Jesus has overcome all the troubles of the world. So even on our worst day—even when we're feeling most defeated—as children of God, as the beloved of a risen Lord, we claim victory as well.

And that deserves a hallelujah—a celebration of a word— no matter how we have to say it.

My "Happy" Ending

So. It's been almost a week since I typed that last sentence. Since—I kid you not—I hit the save button just after I heard something thud and tumble in the basement. It's been a week since I opened my basement door, looked down the stairs, and gasped (okay, and *swore*, if I'm being honest) at the more than three feet of black water that swirled in my basement.

Oh, God, you've got *to be kidding me,* I prayed as I sank on the steps and peeked my head around to see my son's drum kit floating, the overturned tubs of toys out for a swim, my grandmother's chair soaking in sewage.

The rain from the night before had overwhelmed our town's sewers, and they backed up. Into our basement and the basements of hundreds of our neighbors.

It's been almost a week of tossing out heirloom furniture and Christmas decorations, of bleaching vats of toys, of trying to save pieces of my kids' artwork. It's been a week of 90-plus degree temps with 80 percent humidity and no air-conditioning (the waters killed that, too).

It's been a bad week in many ways. While it turns out that insurance will pay for a chunk of the damage, it *is* only a chunk. We've lost a lot. We can't afford to replace most of it. In fact, much is irreplaceable, even if we could afford it. And I've fallen so far behind—on this project, on a talk I'm supposed to be preparing, on my "day" job. And it's so stinking hot. We're so tired. And sweaty. And dirty. And crabby.

But the weird thing is, it's been an amazing week in most other ways. It's been full of friends stopping by to help, to drop off meals. Of family helping to pitch out stuff. It's been full of neighborhood commiseration—which, strangely, I always love.

Mostly, it's been amazing because I found Jesus. Literally. Let me explain: a few years ago, we lost the baby Jesus from our crèche. We searched high and low, to no avail. We prayed that God would help us find Jesus. He didn't. In the Christmases since we lost him, we've used a peanut in place of baby Jesus. It was kind of funny at first, but it didn't really work. The kids were always bummed that we'd lost him. Especially since the set was their dad's as a kid.

Turns out, Jesus had fallen out of the box on the shelves in the furnace room where we keep our Christmas stuff. I know

this now because just the other day after we had emptied
the room of its quickly molding contents, I got down on my
hands and knees on the damp, cold floor and shined a flashlight into the creepy, murky space beneath these shelves.

I pulled out old tiles, a bucket of rusted nails (always nice
to stumble upon), and a whole lot of black gunk. I don't
even want to know what that was. But after I got the gunk
out, I saw something else. It looked toy-like, so I
reached for it.

I turned the flashlight toward my hand, and
when I opened my fist, there was a gunky baby
Jesus. I found Jesus in the dark, murky mess.

I found Jesus in the dark, murky mess.

Duh. We should've looked there years ago. Because that's
always where we can find Jesus, of course. Sometimes I think
God is just nuts for the ways he chooses to remind us of this.

Gunky Jesus

After a good cleaning with bleach and Lysol, I tucked Jesus
into my pocket and took him outside with me to sort through
boxes. I couldn't stop smiling. Not just because the kids were
so excited. But because God is so good.

My task for that day was not easy. Sorting through those
boxes was tough. I was tossing away things—family tokens,
childhood memories—that I'd taken in when my parents split
up and sold their house. I'd clung to these things even as my
family slipped out of my grasp.

I went through old financial documents—reminding me
again of how far we'd "fallen." I saw pictures of my husband
and I—much younger, smilier, in days when we couldn't
even imagine having a pebbly marriage, let alone a jagged

and rocky one. I found old letters and cards we'd sent to one another, full of love and hope and promise.

I sorted through baby toys and clothes—things my kids have loved and looked darling playing with and in.

I picked out a few things to try and save and then chucked the rest into bag after bag after bag. In many ways I trashed the things of my life I had still been holding on to.

It felt great. Freeing. Though I now have less, I have more abundance.

I just watched a garbage truck lift and dump probably thirty bags of stuff (sorry, Earth!), plus the first sofa my husband and I bought together; an antique coffee table I'd salvaged back in college; a chair my grandmother had bought in the 1940s; stuffed animals I'd had since I was a girl; rugs that once lay across my parents' old, elegant dining room, the one where we once had so many happy family holidays. . . .

When the truck hauled the stuff away, I thought I'd cry. But I didn't. It all seemed so—I don't know—strangely dim.

To paraphrase Susan Isaacs: in many ways, God has trashed my life. He flooded and flushed stuff out that didn't need to be there. He pulled out the rugs. He tore out the drywall. He forced me into places where I had to deal with the hurt and disappointment of life. Because when I told him I wanted to follow him and live for him, I asked him to do this.

In the past week, the same thing has happened. The flood has forced me to part with stuff that held me back, that still held me in some sort of grip, that still chained me. The flood freed me to find Jesus in the gunk. And to keep seeking Jesus in the mess.

This is what living salty and shiny is all about. We live knowing that Jesus is there. With us. And we shine. We see floods as chances to clear out and let others help. To reflect back on how many prayers God has answered and to trust that if he's not showing up yet, he will.

Can you imagine if we had found baby Jesus when we first prayed? If God had let me know best? Can you imagine what we'd have lost out on? Wow.

My friend Sarah—who rode her bike over to help us haul stuff on day one of the flood—just told me that my "calmness" amazed her. "I wouldn't be so relaxed with all my belongings in my backyard," she said.

I laughed it off at the time, saying I'd had my moments (and I *have* had a couple of meltdowns). But the truth is, I do feel calm. Because if there's one thing I've learned over the past few grueling years, it's what the old song says, "Life is worth the living just because he lives."[43]

If God can use me best broke and struggling, if he can use me best hurting and tired, if he can use me best flooded or hot, then that's how I want to be used. That's how I want to live. That's the siding I want his light to shine through; that's the flavor of salt I want to add to this world.

It's terrifying to type this. Right now the drywall guys are sawing and hammering (or something) right below me. I'm half expecting something to catch fire (better back this up quick!). That seems to be the way God has been working lately.

But even that—even worse!—wouldn't change how we're to live. We're called to show the light of Christ in this world.

Ever since I wrote about the "race" passage in Hebrews

12:1-3, I've had a lingering nervousness about the word *joy* in that Scripture. You know, where it says, "Because of the joy awaiting [Jesus], he endured the cross, disregarding its shame."

I worry because I've heard it get misinterpreted to reinforce a certain Christian—um, well—lie that we like to tell, which is this: Sure, you've had troubles before, but if you accept Jesus as your Lord and Savior and he lives in your heart, then because of the Cross, joy now awaits you. Essentially, you'll be all happy, happy smiles all the time. You'll be free from your addictions, cured from your diseases, and all your bad relationships will turn out peachy.

I know no one actually *says* it quite like this. But we tend to perpetuate those stories of people who have experienced conversions followed by all sorts of miracles. I'm not saying they don't happen. Certainly they do. But we "forget" to balance them out with the stories of people who "found Jesus" and then got divorced, started smoking, lost their houses, and started on antidepressants. Even though plenty of those exist as well. Visit any 12-step program and you'll hear these stories like crazy. Worse even. Or maybe *better even* is the better way to describe them.

Because the thing of it is, life isn't rosy just because we have Jesus. The Cross gives us hope and grace and a promise of joy in the next life, but not necessarily now. Since you're reading this book, you know it. You get that Jesus meant it when he said, "Here on earth you will have many trials and sorrows" (John 16:33). Because you've lived it.

Don't forget what Jesus said next, though: "But take heart, because I have overcome the world." Living salty and shiny shows that we believe this part. It's because we know he's overcome the world—that he still reigns no matter what—that we choose to press on and live well, live right even in the midst of hardship and hurt and horror. That we allow our light to shine through every old and new hurt, every gaping wound. Even as life tumbles all around us, we still strive to follow and live like Jesus: being loving, kind, graceful, merciful, compassionate, forgiving, just, patient, truthful, trustworthy.

For you, living salty and shiny may mean you show up at your 12-step meeting because Jesus has overcome the world. You don't take that drink or head to the gambling boats because Jesus has overcome the world. Maybe you don't yell at your kids or bad-mouth your spouse or fudge on your taxes because Jesus has overcome the world. You don't pass on that juicy bit of gossip because Jesus has overcome the world. You don't take or get jealous of what isn't yours because Jesus has overcome the world.

You let the light of Jesus shine through; you let the hurt and pain of your life be the salt—flavor!—of the world. That way others see what Jesus can do, which is not make you fakey-happy, creepy-smiley all the time, but make you radiant with God's goodness, grace, and love.

It's *that* that makes us want to celebrate this life. That makes us need to give God our hallelujahs, any way they come. Grumble them, whine them, cry them, shout them, sing them, twirl to them, write them, play them, whisper them, sign them. But offer them.

That's living salty and shiny. That's how you love your life. Hallelujah!

OKAY, GOD:

I've been covered in gook for far too long. I want to shine for you. I want to add flavor to this world for you. Let my story and my experience and my heartaches and my disappointments become something that can honor you in every way.

Anyhow, God, Hallelujah.

Amen.

Getting to Hallelujah

Questions for Reflection and Discussion

1. How well do you think you let Jesus' light shine through your weaknesses? Explain.

2. What has been the effect whenever you've done this?

3. In what ways do your sufferings "salt" or add flavor to this world?

4. How have you seen God at work—or found the gunky Jesus—in the messes of your life? What is better now that you've suffered?

5. What ways and in what places might God be asking you to shine especially brightly for him?

EPILOGUE

UNLESS YOU'RE A WRITER YOURSELF, it's hard to capture and share the thrill of typing the final words in the last chapter. When I chose *Hallelujah* as mine, I was shouting it as I punched the keys. Writing is wonderful and horrible and exhilarating and exhausting all at the same time. So it's nice to be done.

Except the thing about a book like this is that it's never really done. I mean, it's done because I've got a deadline and I just can't keep writing forever. But it's not done because life keeps going, things keep happening, God keeps speaking, ideas keep coming.

Like when my mom called the other morning and mentioned how she was going to throw away two bags of stuff because she'd heard that "throwing or giving away two bags of stuff every day makes your life better."

I heard that and thought, *Oh, shoot. That's good.* Suddenly, I wished I'd had a Live Uncluttered chapter (not that I know anything about this!).

Then I heard my friend Mike preach on worry.

Oh, shoot! Duh. Worry! Why don't I have "Live Worry-Free"?

It was downhill after that. For days all I could think about were the chapters I didn't write that I probably should have—could have. Live Fruitful. Live Forgiven. Live Prayerful. Live Blessed. Live Smart. Live Good.

We should Live Love and know that "Love is patient and kind. Love is not jealous or boastful or proud or rude. It does not demand its own way. It is not irritable, and it keeps no record of being wronged. It does not rejoice about injustice but rejoices whenever the truth wins out. Love never gives up, never loses faith, is always hopeful, and endures through every circumstance" (1 Corinthians 13:4-7).

As my brain ran through the things I may have missed, I grabbed a file full of my earliest notes for this project. I flipped through my random notes—jotted on church bulletins, gum wrappers, pages ripped out of coloring books—and saw all the things that didn't end up in the book. I noticed all the Scripture passages that weren't included.

For a minute.

Leonardo da Vinci said, "Art is never finished, only abandoned." While I'm not sure I'm comfortable calling this book "art" (I think of nonfiction mostly as craft sort of speckled with art), da Vinci's wisdom applies here. I could always tweak, always add. Every day will bring new stories to tell (ooh—like the one about my maple tree that I'm dying to share!). All this because life keeps going. Because I keep learning. Because God keeps revealing.

But that's the good news. While I am going to "abandon" this project, we're all still charged with the task of loving the lives that God has for us. What I've shared with you here are the things that I've needed to work through during the past several years. And they're things I've seen other people in my life working through as well.

What I've written here, however, isn't the end-all. You may have other things you need to work on. So do I, actually. That unclutter thing really got me. And a new crop of fear amid a fuller understanding of my calling have popped up.

So please keep seeking what God wants from you and your life and what you need to do to get there. How do you need to live to love this life? The rest of the story is up to you.

And now, for a benediction stolen from the Franciscans:

May God bless you with discomfort
At easy answers, half-truths, and superficial relationships
So that you may live deep within your heart.

May God bless you with anger
At injustice, oppression, and exploitation of people,
So that you may work for justice, freedom, and peace.

May God bless you with tears
To shed for those who suffer pain, rejection, hunger, and war,
So that you may reach out your hand to comfort them and
To turn their pain into joy.

And may God bless you with enough foolishness
To believe that you can make a difference in the world,
So that you can do what others claim cannot be done
To bring justice and kindness to all our children and the poor.
Amen.

DON'T BE SCARED

Some More Words on Fear from the Bible

ONE OF MY FAVORITE THINGS about angels—and I like a lot of things about angels—is the way they show up to Bible folk. I love that the angels pop out from behind nothing—"suddenly appear"—all ablaze with the glory of God, terrifying those who can see them. And then the angels say—still ablaze with all that glory, still having just popped out of nowhere—"Don't be afraid."

Oh, okay.

It's just so great. And so like God. To put something dazzlingly terrifying in front of you and to say, "Don't be scared."

Oh, okay.

But because he probably isn't sending Gabriel or one of his colleagues to remind you not to be scared, it's helpful to have a good handle on the places and ways that God reminds you that no matter what you face—no matter how strong your enemies, how tough the battle, or how difficult the calling appears to be—God is with you. No need to be afraid.

Simple as that. Easy-peasy, right? Okay, so maybe most of the time it's not simple and it's not easy. As I spent the last year thinking about what keeps me from loving the life God gave me, I realized that fear is behind much of it—whether it's fear that I will have to give up what's most important to me; that others will think less of me; or that God won't come through for me. When fear creeps back in, I need good reminders of God's power, presence, and peace. So I go to the verses below. (For more, visit www.carynrivadeneira.com.) While what scares us may differ from what scared people in Bible times, the principles remain the same. Do not fear. God is with us.

Read on and don't be scared.

God heard the boy crying, and the angel of God called to Hagar from heaven, "Hagar, what's wrong? Do not be afraid! God has heard the boy crying as he lies there."
(Genesis 21:17)

When you go out to fight your enemies and you face horses and chariots and an army greater than your own, do not be afraid. The LORD your God, who brought you out of the land of Egypt, is with you! (Deuteronomy 20:1)

This is my command—be strong and courageous! Do not be afraid or discouraged. For the LORD your God is with you wherever you go. (Joshua 1:9)

Do not be afraid! Don't be discouraged by this mighty army, for the battle is not yours, but God's. (2 Chronicles 20:15)

God is our refuge and strength, a very present help in trouble. Therefore we will not fear though the earth gives way, though the mountains be moved into the heart of the sea.
(Psalm 46:1-2, ESV)

Do not be afraid of the terrors of the night, nor the arrow that flies in the day. (Psalm 91:5)

Say to those with fearful hearts, "Be strong, and do not fear, for your God is coming to destroy your enemies. He is coming to save you." (Isaiah 35:4)

Fear not, for I am with you; be not dismayed, for I am your God; I will strengthen you, I will help you, I will uphold you with my righteous right hand. . . . For I, the LORD your God, hold your right hand; it is I who say to you, "Fear not, I am the one who helps you." (Isaiah 41:10, 13, ESV)

But now, O Jacob, listen to the LORD who created you. O Israel, the one who formed you says, "Do not be afraid, for I have ransomed you. I have called you by name; you are mine." (Isaiah 43:1)

Do not tremble; do not be afraid. Did I not proclaim my purposes for you long ago? You are my witnesses—is there any other God? No! There is no other Rock—not one! (Isaiah 44:8)

Yes, you came when I called; you told me, "Do not fear." (Lamentations 3:57)

Are not two sparrows sold for a penny? And not one of them will fall to the ground apart from your Father. But even the hairs of your head are all numbered. Fear not, therefore; you are of more value than many sparrows. (Matthew 10:29-31, ESV)

Fear not, little flock; for it is your Father's good pleasure to give you the kingdom. (Luke 12:32, KJV)

About the Author

CARYN DAHLSTRAND RIVADENEIRA might spend more time thinking, dreaming, and plotting than she does actually writing. But since it's the writing part that pays (some of, at least) the bills, she calls herself a writer. Oh, and a speaker. And an editor. Definitely a mother. And a wife. It gets so complicated.

Caryn is the author of *Mama's Got a Fake I.D.* (WaterBrook Press, 2009) and *Grumble Hallelujah* and the former editor of *Marriage Partnership*, *Christian Parenting Today*, and *Gifted for Leadership*, all parts of Christianity Today International (CTI). Caryn continues her role with CTI as a regular contributor to *Kyria*, *Gifted for Leadership*, and the *Her.Meneutics* blog.

Caryn has written dozens of magazine articles for such publications as *Christianity Today*, *Neue*, *FamilyLife*, and *Engineering and Mining Journal* (you read that right), and of course in the publications she edited. Caryn and her Mommy Revolution blog cofounder, Carla Barnhill, were columnists for *Today's Christian Woman* magazine.

Caryn leads workshops and speaks at conferences and church groups across the country. She's been a repeat guest on Moody Radio's *Midday Connection* with Anita Lustrea and Melinda Schmidt. She has been on such radio shows as *The John and Kathy Show*, *Changing Worldviews/WOMANTalk* with Sharon Hughes, *I Thought She Said* with Faith Daly, *The Paul Edwards Program*, and *Talk from the Heart* with Rich Buhler. Caryn has also appeared on *The Harvest Show*.

Caryn is a founding member of the Redbud Writers Guild, a group of Christian women writers in Chicagoland committed to expanding the female voice in their communities, churches, and culture.

Caryn earned a B.A. in English from Calvin College and attended the University of Chicago's publishing program. She lives in Chicago's western suburbs with her husband, Rafael; her three kids (Henrik [9], Greta [7], and Fredrik [4]); and their rescued pit bull terrier. They are members of Elmhurst Christian Reformed Church.

Visit Caryn at www.carynrivadeneira.com. Find her on Facebook at facebook.com/carynrivadeneira and on Twitter @CarynRivadeneir.

Acknowledgments

IN MOST WAYS, writing is a lonely business—just the writer and her wacky little thoughts. But if the writer is honest, she starts to recognize that many of the thoughts (especially the less wacky ones) and ideas and images began dog-paddling around in her noggin because someone else introduced them in some way, shape, or form.

That's certainly been the case with this book. Just days after I got the idea to write a book based on my "I hate my life" moment, I sat in a backyard with my friend Kim. At the time, Kim was facing down things no thirtysomething woman should have to face: infertility, breast cancer, depression. And yet, after sharing some of her struggles, in one shining moment, Kim said, "But I don't know. I just love my life."

Though that story doesn't appear in this book (now I'm wondering why not), her words changed my life and started my quest to find out how I could love my life too. Thanks, Kim.

But I can't forget these folks, either. Thanks to:

Leonard Cohen for writing "Hallelujah." I've read that you think the song is way overplayed—and it may be—but if it didn't play on Pandora.com that day, I might have missed it when I needed it. It inspired my title and gave my emotions a melody.

My "pastor friends" Tracey, Gregg, and Mike. Were you not in my life, I might have to go to seminary.

My small-groupy-type-thing (I told you we needed a name for what we are!). Rachel, Mark, Stacie, Dave, Sarah, Gregg, Jennifer, and Brian, your friendship is one of my new favorite parts of life.

My writers group, Redbud Writers Guild (www.redbudwritersguild .com). Thanks for your support and feedback on this project. I love you and am so grateful God brought us together to share our writing, wanna-change-the-world lives.

My Facebook friends and Twitter followers who answered "research" questions when I asked and offered other insights unknowingly.

My babysitters (er, my kids' babysitters), especially Mary Ellen and my fantastic in-laws, Rafael and Lourdes. No way I could've written a book over the summer without you!

Denise and Bethany, thanks for all the double dirty skim chais and for keeping my reading list up-to-date and for keeping me laughing while I "worked" in the coffee shop.

Sarah Atkinson, my acquisitions editor at Tyndale House. Thanks not only for championing my book but naming my (yes, *my!*) future manor house, as well.

Kim Miller, my "regular" editor at Tyndale House. It's always terrifying handing off your manuscript to somebody. I can't imagine this having been in any better hands. You made this book better.

Other fine Tyndale folk: Jan Long Harris, Nancy Clausen, Yolanda Sidney, Bonne Steffen, and Beth Sparkman. What a stellar team you Knox folks are. You're such joys to work with.

My agent, Andrea Heinecke. You stepped in the middle of this and handled it like you cradled it since infancy. Thanks for that!

Of course, I need to thank my family. To Mom and Dad, thanks for all your love and encouragement through the years. I love you both and am grateful for the tools you gave me to live life well.

To my husband, Rafi, thanks for your patience with me and your unwavering support of my calling. Thanks for being a model of courage and living with principles. (Shoot! That would've been a good chapter!) In a world where most people live—and stand—for nothing, you shoot for what is right. I love you for that.

And to my kids, Henrik, Greta, and Fredrik. It can't be easy to have a mom who writes stories about the family. Kind of mortifying, actually. Thanks for loving me anyway. I love you guys.

Oh, and God: thanks for turning my wailing into dancing and my grumbles into this crazy book. Grumble, grumble, hallelujah.

Notes

1. BBC News, "Al Gore: Groomed for Power," December 15, 2002, http://news.bbc.co.uk/2/hi/americas/2327377.stm.
2. Ibid.
3. From a sermon given by Rev. Bert DeJong, senior pastor of Elmhurst Christian Reformed Church in Elmhurst, Illinois.
4. Henri Nouwen, *In Memoriam* (South Bend, IN: Ave Maria Press, 2005), 42.
5. James Herriot, *Favorite Dog Stories* (New York: St. Martin's Press, 1995), 5.
6. George Gershwin and Ira Gershwin, "Stiff Upper Lip," 1937.
7. Bob Hyatt, "Don't Forget to Grieve," *Out of Ur* (blog), March 31, 2010, http://www.outofur.com/archives/2010/03/dont_forget_to.html.
8. "Crying," Wikipedia, http://en.wikipedia.org/wiki/Crying.
9. If you need one, check out R. S. Jones's "Shelter" in *Unleashed: Poems by Writers' Dogs*, edited by Amy Hempel and Jim Shepard (New York: Three Rivers Press, 2005), 102.
10. *Merriam-Webster's Collegiate Dictionary*, 11th ed., s.v. "lament."
11. From a sermon given by Rev. Gregg DeMey at Elmhurst Christian Reformed Church on March 14, 2010.
12. Chapin Hartford and Sarah Hart, "Better Than a Hallelujah," Spiritandsong.com.
13. From a sermon given by Rev. Gregg DeMey at Elmhurst Christian Reformed Church on February 28, 2010.
14. Susan E. Isaacs, *Angry Conversations with God: A Snarky but Authentic Spiritual Memoir* (Nashville: FaithWords, 2009), 221.
15. This article, "Surviving Stuck," first appeared on Kyria.com. Used by permission of Christianity Today International, Carol Stream, IL 60188.
16. Marshall Shelley, "The 'Eighth Deadly Sin' Revisited," *Leadership Weekly* (March 28, 2001), http://www.christianitytoday.com/le /currenttrendscolumns/leadershipweekly/cln10328.html.
17. Donald Miller, *A Million Miles in a Thousand Years: What I Learned While Editing My Life* (Nashville: Thomas Nelson, 2009), 115–116.
18. Ibid., 108.
19. Sandra Boyton, *Dog Train: A Wild Ride on the Rock-and-Roll Side* (New York: Workman Publishing Co., 2005).
20. Thanks to Mary DeMuth for tweeting this little beauty. It's from *My Utmost for His Highest*, "The Staggering Question," June 1, http://www.myutmost.org /06/0601.html.
21. See Matthew 25:14-30.
22. See Luke 1:13, NIV.
23. Carla Barnhill, "Carla Is Jealous of Your Facebook Status," *The Mommy Revolution* (blog), August 11, 2010, http://www.themommyrevolution.com.

24. Ibid.

25. Dick Towner and John Tofilon, *Good Sense Budget Course* (Grand Rapids: Zondervan and Willow Creek Association, 2002), 170.

26. She later e-mailed me to attribute this to Charles Williams.

27. Linda Buturian, "Prefer the Given," *Christian Century* online, *Theolog*, February 18, 2009, http://christiancentury.blogspot.com/2009/02 /prefer-given.html.

28. *Merriam-Webster*, 11th ed., s.v. "mercy."

29. In this passage, Paul quotes from Deuteronomy 32:35.

30. And Donald Miller, apparently, since he talks about the study in *A Million Miles in a Thousand Years*. I'd cite him on this, except I wrote about it before coming across it in his book. I was delighted to read about it yet again.

31. See http://themommyrevolution.wordpress.com/about/.

32. Todd Hertz, "Communicating That Fringe Benefits Are Just That," ThinkChristian (blog), June 22, 2010, http://www.thinkchristian.net/index .php/2010/06/22/communicating-that-fringe-benefits-are-just-that/.

33. Sandra Westfall, "John Edwards's Daughter: Our Lives Were 'Savaged,'" *People*, http://www.people.com/people/article/0,,20397371,00.html.

34. *Norton Anthology of English Literature*, 5th ed. (New York: W. W. Norton & Company, 1987), 1100.

35. Camerin Courtney, "The Gift of Doubt," *Today's Christian Woman* (March/ April 2006), http://www.kyria.com/topics/spiritualformation /theologyspiritualissues/1.18.html.

36. Susan E. Isaacs, *Angry Conversations with God*, 238.

37. R. Kelso Carter in *Promises of Perfect Love* by John Sweney and Kelso Carter (Philadelphia, PA: John J. Hood, 1886).

38. Judy Douglass, "Waiting with Hope—A Study on Psalm 27," Thoughts about God, http://www.thoughts-about-god.com/biblestudies/jd-psalms27.htm. Used with permission.

39. Parker Palmer, "The Shadow of My Hand on the Paper: Writing and Living a Life," April 17, 2010, lecture at the Festival of Faith & Writing, Calvin College, Grand Rapids, Michigan.

40. *Johnny Cash's America*, Morgan Neville and Robert Gordon, directors, Sony Legacy, 2008.

41. "For the Childless Woman on Mother's Day," *The Wisdom Tree* (blog), May 8, 2009, http://vinitawright.typepad.com/my_weblog/2009/05/for-the -childless-woman-on-mothers-day.html.

42. Shauna Niequist, *Bittersweet: Thoughts on Change, Grace, and Learning the Hard Way* (Grand Rapids: Zondervan, 2010), 248.

43. Words and music by William J. and Gloria Gaither, "Because He Lives," copyright © 1971.

? **ALL THE WRONG QUESTIONS** 4

WITHDRAWN

Why are the snacks so terrible?

Why are we stopping?

What's the rest of the story?

ALL THE WRONG QUESTIONS

"Who Could That Be at This Hour?"
"When Did You See Her Last?"
"Shouldn't You Be in School?"
"Why Is This Night Different from All Other Nights?"

ADDITIONAL REPORTS

File Under: 13 Suspicious Incidents